This collection consists of three characteristic new plays, as yet unperformed, by the great Irish dramatist whose eightieth birthday was celebrated in 1960. The plays are in the true O'Casey tradition, a grand mixture of fantasy, outrageous farce, satire, symbolism, melodrama, expressionism, song, dance — all these dissimilar elements being woven together with the author's peculiar skill. The central theme is a favourite of the older O'Casey : let us choose life and youth and song, and pit their buoyant strength against the forces of death and rusty age and tears ; let us love life, not just endure it.

The green curtains of the title-play, a three-act piece, symbolise the obscurantism and humbug of Irish Catholicism which the author attacks with his still glorious use of language.

In *Figuro in the Night*, a short play in two scenes set in Dublin, he again fires off a fusillade at the puritanism of the Irish church and makes a strong plea for pagan freedom. The piece is notable for the vividness of the prose-poetry in the dialogue.

The Moon Shines on Kylenamoe is a short, light, almost farcical comedy set in a lonely Irish railway station at night, and should be welcome wherever one-act plays are performed and Irish accents available.

BEHIND THE GREEN CURTAINS

FIGURO IN THE NIGHT

THE MOON SHINES
ON KYLENAMOE

Three Plays

BY

SEAN O'CASEY

ST MARTIN'S PRESS
NEW YORK

CONTENTS

The music for the incidental songs is to be found on pages 159-164

BEHIND THE GREEN CURTAINS

' The business of a Journalist is to destroy the truth, to lie out-
right, to pervert, to vilify, to fawn at the feet of Mammon, and to sell
himself, his country, and his race for his daily bread. We are the
tools of rich men behind the scenes.' — Pronouncement by John
Swinton, Editor *New York Times*, at a banquet given to mark his
retirement, and quoted in *The Irish Press*, October 10, 1959, from the
Autumn No. of *Writer's Digest*.

And the reviewer asks : ' What are the words of a man speaking
as a journalist doing in a periodical publishing the words of men
functioning as writers ? '

As if journalists weren't writers, too ! They are the most influ-
ential of all, for these are they who speak, not only to some of the
people all the time, or all the people some of the time, but to all the
people all the time. Therefore are they very dangerous if so be they
refuse to walk, not within the light — for few of us do or can — but
within the shadow of truth, courage, and sincerity.

> Ah, my heart is weary all alone
> And it sends a lonely cry
> To the land that sings beyond my dreams
> And the lonely Sundays pass me by.
>   Ah, the quiet land of Erin.

THE JITTERING GATE

A part of a residential district. It is part street and part a churchyard attached to the Protestant Church of St. Ashlingoch. There is two-thirds of a house, two-storey, seen to the left, with three small windows on upper storey and two larger ones below, between which is a doorway. The left larger window on ground floor is filled by a picture showing the head of a bearded man, thoughtful and stern : it is surrounded by a frame of vivid green bunting. A festoon of yellow and white bunting stretches from the left window of upper storey, looped up at the second, and fastened to the third window on the right. From the side of this house go railings bordering the churchyard to a church porch at the very right ; a little way from this porch is a narrow gateway to the churchyard ; in the middle of this gateway is a cross from which the pattern branches. At the moment, the gateway is shut. In front of the porch, partly hiding it, are a few trees, little more than saplings, but leafy. The outlines of the scene, railings, house, porch, and trees, take somewhat the look of a sketch, as if the objects were seen through an early morning, or late evening, mist, though the picture of the bearded man is fairly clear. The porch door is open, and we hear faintly the music of the 'Dead March' in Saul, played on the organ. It is a very warm afternoon, sunny, the heat so strong that it creates something of a humid mist.

Parallel with the railings is a bench to hold three or four. Two women, Lizzie and Angela, come slowly in ; they walk slow, for the heat has gripped them. Both are just in their middle age, and both have the appearance of one-time hawkers, now, possibly, content to live on their meagre pensions and whatever charitable gifts they can wheedle or scrounge out of others and from charitable societies. They are dressed in faded clothing : one in a black skirt, and brown jacket, with a blue made-up straw hat on her head ; her companion in a brown skirt, with a faded black-and-red-patterned shawl over the head and shoulders. Lizzie is a little in front of Angela, and makes towards the bench ; Angela catches sight of the picture in the window, and goes towards it to have a look. Lizzie, seeing this, halts to take a part in the look, but with far less interest.

Lizzie [*as she comes in*]. This heat's cookin' me. I can't go a step further without restin' me old bones, so I can't.

Angela [*staring at the picture*]. Wondher who he is now ? One o' th' Saints or one o' th' Blesseds ?

Lizzie [*without interest*]. One of th' Blesseds only — 'tisn't coloured.

Angela. Might even be some great bishop.

Lizzie. Couldn't be, woman ; where's his helmet ?

Angela. What helmet, Lizzie ?

Lizzie. You know well enough — them comic consthructions they wear on their heads when they're processin' some particular church doin's.

Angela. Oh, that. No, he hasn't. I'd say it was St. Joseph only for th' beard floatin' too far out on th' sides.

Lizzie. Well, St. Lizzie here is goin' to float over to th' bench for a sit down, an' leave yeh to your studies. [*She does so.*]

Angela. I wondher now : Yis, seein' th' green stuff around it, it might well be some ould Irish saint, banished be time an' disturbance from th' minds o' mortal men.

Lizzie. Aw, pull yourself together, Angela, an' quit sendin' your probin' meditations inta another's head ; stabbin', stabbin' away any quietness that a mind needs on a day like this. [*She cocks an ear to the solemn music trickling from the church porch.*] Aw, that music ! As hot as I am, it sends me shiverin'. [*To Angela*] What kinda stuff is it ?

Angela [*not noticing the question — suddenly and eagerly to Lizzie*]. Eh, remember th' oul' Irish saint that let a bird nest in his beard, an' stood stock still till th' eggs had hatched, and th' chicks reared, an' got th' power to fly away ? What was th' boyo's name, Lizzie ?

Lizzie [*now sitting down on the bench*]. I dunno, an' I don't care, Angela. If yeh don't mind, you'll have a nest in your own oul' nut, hatchin' odd things out'll get yeh inta throuble one day or another. [*Angrily*] Will yeh give over roamin' outa your right mind, an' for God's sake, leave your bearded gent alone in his green battle-ment, an' sit down or go away, for if yeh go on ques-tionin', questionin', you'll question yourself inta a question of whether you are or you aren't ?

Angela [*in deep reflection*]. Where, now, did I see that sterun face before ?

Lizzie [*with irritation*]. Aaw, come an' sit down, an' don't stand fizzin' questions outa yeh with your who-is-its and where-was-its, sendin' them here on a sunbeam, buzzin' me ear, refusin' to hear, but forced to listen all th' time.

Angela [*with certitude*]. I'm as certain I seen, walkin' in some road, sittin' in some place, or presented in a picture, certain as I live that I seen that face before.

Lizzie. If y'ask me, you'll get rid of any wish to see th' oul' gob ever again. Leave it, leave it, girl, an' sit down, an' thry to remember that none of us is a damn bit betther for knowin' things.

    Angela gives a lingering look at the picture, then comes slowly to the bench, and sits down beside her friend.

Angela [*as she sits*]. All th' same, I like siftin' out things.

Lizzie. Well, sift yourself outa th' habit for a few minutes, an' qualify th' hotness o' th' day with quietness. [*She shudders.*] Ugh ! That music stuff gives me th' creeps !

Angela. A dirge.

Lizzie. A what ?

Angela. Some stiff gettin' berried. [*Crossing herself.*] Th' Lord ha' mercy on us all ! [*A silent pause.*] You can hear th' dead bell tollin'.

Lizzie [*listening for a moment*]. Dead bell tollin' ? I hear no bell.

Angela [*beating the slow time with a hand*]. In th' music. Th' beat, like a drum. Dum dum dum. Funeral march.

Lizzie [*irritably*]. Can't you let misery alone without addin' a glitther to it ? Isn't th' plain tune bad enough without puttin' a dhrum into it, with your dum dum dum ! Th' throuble people go to make you more miserable than th' world does ! For God's sake,

Angela, thry to sit still, an' let th' good sun pene-
thrate your vitals in quietness an' peace !

Angela. You do take on !

Lizzie [*angrily*]. Take on ! Whatja mean, take on ?

Angela. 'Bout th' music. It's meant to do it.

Lizzie. Are yeh wandherin', Angela ? Meant to do
what ?

Angela. Why, get yeh down.

Lizzie [*sharply*]. It's something to get us up we want,
Angela, an' not nothin' to get us down !

Angela. I dunno but what a gettin' of us down is a
chance from th' saints to keep us from settlin' down
in a world we have to go from.

Lizzie. Keep yeh from settlin' down — fancy that !

Angela. Well, we can't cling to th' world th' way ivy
clings to a wall.

Lizzie. No ? [*sarcastically*] Is it entherin' an ordher y'are,
or maybe, you've taken up with them lay apostles th'
clergy are always blatherin' about at th' missions ?

Angela [*seriously*]. I wouldn't make fun, Lizzie ; afther
all, there's such a thing as a disappearance.

Lizzie [*irritably*]. Talk plain, woman. Whadja mean,
disappearance ?

Angela. When we go, we disappear ; you disappear an'
I disappear.

Lizzie [*fervently*]. What a pity there's no chance of you
doin' a disappearance now !

Angela. I wouldn't go on mockin' holy things, Lizzie.

Lizzie. Oh, Lord ! Aw, for Jasus' sake, settle down on th' seat, an' give a chance to th' sun to surprise yeh !

Angela [*swaying several times on her seat to give herself an impetus to get up from it*]. God ha' mercy, but I'm gettin' stiff ! [*With a bigger sway, she gets to her feet, goes close to Lizzie, bends over her, and speaks solemnly.*] I don't go an inch before, or remain an inch behind, in me duty to warn yeh, Elizabeth Latterly !

Lizzie [*flabbergasted*]. I dunno, I really dunno. Warn me, is it ? Not a kindly warnin' either, to Lizzie, but a menacin' one to Elizabeth Latterly ! I really dunno. [*Bending towards Angela who has sat down again.*] Warnin' Elizabeth Latterly — against what, woman ?

Angela [*quietly but firmly*]. Lapsin'.

Lizzie [*bewildered and quietly indignant*]. Oh, lapsin'. An' may poor Elizabeth Latterly ask th' kind lady who or what she's lapsin' from ?

Angela [*with a slight hiccup*]. Th' true way, th' faith.

Lizzie [*sitting silent for a few moments ; then she looks closely at Angela, sniffing as she does so. She gets up from the bench, swaying to and fro several times before she manages it, stands in front of Angela, and bends down towards her*]. Now I know. Aren't you th' sly oul' bitch ! Muddlin' again, an' warnin' me against a lapse. I should ha' guessed. Didn't th' two of us, with lighted candles, vow before th' figure of Saint Sinfoilio, that no liquor ud trickle over our lips till such time as the meetin' an' demonsthration for Cardinal Minteyzenty was over an' done with. You an' me, Angela Carrigeen ; an'

now, th' whiff from your breath — whew ! — when the
wind blows this way, is overpowerin'.

Angela [*a little tearfully, with another slight hiccup*]. You
have th' gift of lowerin' more than a sup yourself,
Lizzie Lattherly.

Lizzie. But I don't thry to deceive th' blessed saints ; I
stick to me undertakin'. I can dhrink more'n a sup,
Angela Carrigeen, but I'm not a walkin' tanker of
stout, like some whose name I disdain to mention.
D'ye get that, Angela Carrigeen ? Some whose name I
disdain to mention. And, besides, let me tell you —
[*While she has been speaking, McGeelish has come in, slowly
and rather furtively. He is noticed by the two women, who
pause to watch him. He goes over to the narrow porch, takes
a step to go inside, hesitates, then retreats. Continuing*] An'
let me tell yeh, Angela Carrigeen, that Lizzie Lattherly
whatever th' quantity and measurement of sups she
consumes [*she pauses to look at McGeelish who has stolen to
the narrow gateway*], she keeps an even keel, an' an
avowal made before a saintly figure an' a lighted candle
is a matther I wouldn't introduce to a conthradiction ;
[*she pauses again to watch McGeelish slink away from the
gateway, passing by them as he goes out*] not for a china jar
o' wine from Rome's Royal Pope ; no, nor for a full
vat of Guinness's Three Star stout !

Angela. Three Ex stout, yeh mean. [*She looks at Lizzie
suspiciously, who suddenly gives a slight hiccup, and steps
unsteadily back to the bench.*] Oh ho, your mind's mixin'
stars with exes.

Lizzie. Me many words staggered me breath. I'm not
one given to tellin' lies.

Angela. If y' ask me, you're no specialitee at tellin' th' thruth.

Lizzie [*making a little unsteadily for the bench*]. It's no secret, ma'am. [*She sits down suddenly with a flop.*] Oh ! I'm a Hi-Fi when it comes to makin' a [*she gives a slight hiccup*] vow ! [*A pause.*] Wondher what that eejut was doin' nosin' round th' gateway ?

Angela [*pleadingly*]. Listen, Lizzie : I won a few quid in th' Pools, an' I lost me head.

Lizzie. An' kept it quiet ; all to yourself. Yeh went to bed with it an' got up with it, an' didn't give a hint of it even to th' image in your lookin'-glass that only showed yourself.

Angela. I'm weak, Lizzie ; I admit it ; all women is.

Lizzie. Speak for yourself, Angela Carrigeen, an' leave present company out, please. Oh, there's th' damned thing again !
  [*It is the ' Dead March ' in* Saul *that she hears again, trickling out from the church. The Verger is seen behind the railings. He wears a long black gown, with black velvet collar to shoulder. He comes to the narrow gateway, unlocks it, and comes from the churchyard, shutting and locking the gateway after him. He faces towards the porch, sights the two women, and greets them.*]

Verger. Good morning, ladies.

Lizzie [*surprised — hesitantly*]. Good mornin', sir.
  As the Verger appears, and is locking the gateway, Dan Basawn opens the door of the house, stands in the doorway smoking a pipe. He is about 40, beginning to

*grow grey on the head, moustache, and a straggly tuft of
whiskers on his chin. He is wearing no coat ; light-blue
check shirt which has a yellow and white ribbon-rosette
pinned on it to the left ; ordinary rough tweed trousers.
He goes over to the bench and sits on end farthest from
the two women, puffing his pipe, watching women and
Verger. Beoman takes a place in doorway, smoking a pipe
too. A taller man, nearing 30, dressed in dungarees,
but with a vivid handkerchief round his neck, and a bowler
hat on his head, worn at a rakish angle.*

Verger [*stretching out his arms as if greeting the fine day,
lilting*]. Oh, what a beautiful mornning !

Lizzie [*surprised*]. Eh ?

Verger. Oh, what a beautiful day !

Angela [*moving swiftly to the end of the bench where Lizzie is
sitting, nearest to the Verger*]. I dunno, sir — I'm gaspin' !

Lizzie [*to Angela*]. Have some manners, woman ; go an'
gasp somewhere else. [*To the Verger*] Why're they
playin' what makes a body shiver on a day of resoundin'
sun ?

Verger. Oh, they're just practising 'Dead March' from
Saul before the cortège comes.

Angela [*bending past Lizzie towards the Verger*]. Th' what
comes ?

Beoman [*swiftly whipping pipe from his mouth to speak, crisply
and tersely*]. Th' stiff, ma'am !

Angela [*a little confused with a new voice*]. Oh, yis, yis — th'
stiff ! Exactly !

B.G.C.——B

Verger [*going into the porchway — lilting*] :
>   I've got a wonderful feeling,
>   Everything's going my way !

[*He goes in, shutting porch door behind him, and the music is no longer heard.*

Lizzie [*with a snort of contempt*]. Him an' his God be wi' yeh an' his [*mimicking his lilt*] oh, what a beautiful morning ! His beautiful day is dhryin' me up !

Angela [*in anguish*]. I'm all afire ! You're runnin' a risk, Lizzie ; sunsthroke. I must have a quencher. [*She rises from bench, and stands in front of Lizzie, looking down at her. A pause.*] Have a heart for yourself, an' get undher th' shade of a glass o' plain, Lizzie ; just one, mind you, no more ; I prayed an' prayed to Saint Ishkabaheen for strength—

[*Beoman darts over and takes Angela's place on the bench.*

Lizzie [*interrupting*]. That fella ! He's an idler, if ever there was one. Thump th' sky with prayers, an' he wouldn't take th' least notice, Angela.

Beoman [*with a snort of scorn*]. Pshaw !

Angela. An' then, I thried Saint Pether.

Lizzie. Aw, he's too big an' busy with his keys, shuttin' out an' lettin' in.

Beoman [*whipping the pipe out of his mouth — explosively*]. Dummies.

Angela [*to Lizzie who looks indignantly towards Beoman*]. Never mind him, dear. A Saint has to know your outs an' ins before he gives a beck ; a Blessed buzzes down, all ears, minute he hears his name mentioned. What I say is that th' Saints get kinda stuck-up, y'know, an' th' one chance a body has is with th' Blesseds.

Lizzie. Don't I know it ! Th' Blesseds has to keep on their toes to get notice, if they .wants to be hoisted up into higher places.

Angela. Yis, among th' cymbals an' th' dhrums.

Beoman [*with a snort of scorn*]. Th' harps an' th' hoboes — a Phil th' Fluther's Ball !

Lizzie [*leaning close to Beoman and putting her face close to his*]. Bah !

Angela [*pulling her gently away*]. Never heed him, dearie. A runt in mind an' a runt in manners. Come, Lizzie, or we'll just dissolve inta a doctor's prescription !

Lizzie. Awright, but remember, one glass for me ; no more ; taken gently an' let go down with caution. One only ; not a single another I vow that — I vow !

Angela. An' oney two for me ; I vow it ; an' taken down sip be sip, mind yeh.

Lizzie. Yis, sip be sip be sip.

Angela [*as they go out slowly*]. Sip sip sip. [*Suddenly halting opposite the picture in the house window.*] I take me solemn word that that's St. Joseph !

Lizzie. I'd say it was meant for St. Pether.

Angela. Aw, no ; th' beard isn't fluffy enough, Lizzie ; not half fluffy enough.

Lizzie. Whah'ja mean, fluffy ? St. Pether's beard was bushy, woman ; never fluffy.

Angela. You'll have to give in, it bulged a lot.

Lizzie [*indignantly*]. Bulged ! Whah'ja mean, bulged ? It fitted his face, didn' it ? St. Pether's beard was trimmed etiquettishly as th' beard of any of your grandees.

Angela [*suddenly darting a little nearer to the men on the bench*]. Eh, either of yous know [*pointing towards picture*], is that a picture of St. Joseph or St. Pether ?

Beoman [*with vicious emphasis*]. A betther man than either of them. [*Explosively*] PARNELL !

Lizzie. You shouldn' ask questions of positive sthrangers, — them swagger-mouths is part of the scenery now ;
      They're like th' black flies
      Comin' outa the skies,
      Doin' damage an' harm
      Till th' lot o' them dies !
[*Pulling Angela along*] We're wastin' time ; come on, if you're comin'.

Angela [*as they go*]. Mind you, one for you, two for me ; we vowed, no more ; lowered slow ; sip, sip.

Lizzie [*as they go off*]. Sip sip sip.

Basawn [*reprovingly — to Beoman*]. It's a wondher you'd batther two ignoran' oul' women with your insinuatin' disbelief. [*A pause, Beoman remaining silent.*] Hurtin' th' lovely day that's in it be your irreverent snorts. [*Another pause.*] It's a standin' wondher to me how anybody can dive or dip inta snortin' at a faith that has th' Christian world sizzlin' with miracles !

Beoman. Sizzlin', eh ? With miracles ? [*Explosively*] Where !

Basawn. Everywhere : Lourdes, Fatima, Knock.

Beoman. Fruitin' loud an' useless prayers, last hopes, an' vain yearnin's.

Basawn. I suppose you'd dispute th' weepin' Statue of th' Blessed Virgin of Syracuse, too ?

Beoman. Never heard tell of it.

Basawn. 'Course yeh didn't. Well, all Italy's talkin' about it, newspapers an' priests ; crowds pressin' to see it, th' Blessed Statue weepin' big tears with them as knows declarin' them human dhrops.

Beoman. Oh yeah ?

Basawn [*vehemently*]. Yes, oh yeah ! Weepin' she was because another woman was weepin', too.

Beoman. Then she'll be workin' well inta th' night if she weeps for every woman who's weepin', too !

Basawn. This was a special occasion : th' woman had a special reason for weepin'.

Beoman. Are yeh talkin' now of th' Statue or th' woman ?

Basawn [*irritably*]. I'm talkin' of both, but it was the woman who was weepin'.

Beoman. You said a second ago that both of them was weepin' at th' same time.

Basawn. Th' woman started it first an' then th' Blessed Statue joined in.

Beoman. Why ?

Basawn. Ah, why what ?

Beoman. Why was th' Statue weepin' ? It's no easy thing for any statue to do.

Basawn. Amn't I afther sayin' that th' woman was weepin' because her husband was a Communist, an' when th' Blessed Statue noticed it, th' Statue began its weepin', too.

Beoman. Yes, but was she weepin' for the one, or was she weepin' for th' other, or was she weepin' for both ?

Basawn. What one an' what other an' what both are yeh talkin' about ?

Beoman. It musta been one or t'other or both.

   [*Bunny, McGeelish, McGeera, Horawn, a girl, and some others, actors and writers, have come in ; have gone to the porch, hesitated, and retreated to the gateway, clustering around it. The two men on the bench cease talking to watch them, resuming their talk when the others have clustered round the gateway.*

Basawn [*resuming discussion*]. Listen ta me : I'll lay it out in divisions so's you won't put a tangle inta th' consequence. Th' woman was in her home in Syracuse. Th' woman was weepin', an' she was weepin' because her husband was a Communist ; th' Blessed Statue seein' her weepin' began her weepin', too, so that th' Blessed Statue plus th' woman was weepin' together ; an' both were weepin' because th' woman's husband who was weepin' was a Communist. See ?

Beoman. You've brought another one weepin' inta it now !

Basawn. No such utterance, man, ever penethrated past me lips.

Beoman. Yeh said th' Statue was weepin', th' woman was weepin', and th' husband was weepin' with both o' them.

Basawn. Never ! No, sir ; you're gallivantin' inta a tangle again ; th' Statue an' th' woman was weepin' for th' same reason — because th' woman's husband was a Communist.

Beoman. What did she say ?

Basawn. What did who say ?

Beoman. Th' Statue ?

Basawn. Nothin', man, nothin' !

Beoman. Then how d'yeh know ?

Basawn. How do I know what, man ?

Beoman. How d'yeh know th' Statue was weepin' jus' because th' woman's husband was a Communist ?

Basawn. Holy God, what else could th' sacred Statue have been weepin' for ?

Beoman. It might jus' as well ha' been weepin' because th' woman wasn't a Communist herself.
    [*Chatastray comes running in and over to the group at the gateway, a little out of breath.*

Chatastray. Sorry, lads ; kept be some business. Thought yous have been all in th' church be now. We'll be just in time. Saw th' hearse comin' round th' corner. [*He moves towards the porch.*] Come on, or we'll be late.

McGeelish. Hold on, hold on ; we've been considhering, an' most of us have doubts.

Chatastray [*impatiently*]. We settled all that, didn't we ? We decided, come what would, to attend th' funeral of Lionel Robartes, who was always ready to help young actor and writer ; a famous playwright, a doctor of literature ; a distinguished lecturer ; dammit, we must do it, if we aren't to feel ashamed for th' rest of our lives !

McGeelish. Think o' th' risk : Catholics at a non-Catholic religious Service may incur excommunication.

Bunny. May ? Do, man ; incur it automatically.

Chatastray [*impatiently*]. Oh God, all this over again ! [*Vehemently*] Are we going or are we not ?

[*A silent pause.*]

Beoman [*lilting softly*] :

So th' old flute was doomed, and its fate was pathetic.
'Twas fasten'd an' burn'd at the stake as heretic.
While th' flames roar'd round it, they heard a strange noise ;
'Twas the old flute still whistlin' ' Th' Protestant Boys ! '

McGeelish [*angrily — to Beoman*]. What th' hell does that mean ?

Beoman. Jus' murmurin' a warnin' that youse might share th' fate of th' old flute.

Chatastray. Now, now, Martin, don't be interferin'. [*To the others — apologetically*] Beoman, my foreman factory engineer. Well, come on in.

Horawn. Wait a minute, wait a minute.

Bunny [*with a sigh*]. If only we had Yeats with us now !

Basawn [*explosively — with scorn and resentment*]. That fella !

Horawn [*impatiently*]. Oh, Yeats again ! We have to live an' fight without him.

Beoman [*with a snort of derision*]. Fight !

Bunny. Ireland misses him sadly.

McGeera [*angrily*]. Misses him ! How in th' name of God ? Makes me mad to see people fancyin' thundher an' lightning in Ireland's sky when th' name of Yeats is mentioned.

McGeelish. He was always a swell. Never had a hard time like us. Half th' world bendin' th' knee to him. Yeats lived behind velvet curtains.

Chatastray. Looka, let's go in or stay out — one thing or th' other : which is it to be ?

McGeelish. Might be wiser to go in casually, one be one, 'stead of pushin' in in a bunch.

Bunny. That's an idea.

Horawn. I bet Kornavaun has an eye on us from some corner or other.

Chatastray. Oh, to hell with Kornavaun ! For God's sake let us go in together.

Beoman [*murmuring mockingly*]. Like th' deer on mountain heather.

Basawn [*to Beoman — sarcastically*]. Funny man !

McGeera. Let one of us prowl a bit to see if th' coast is clear.

Bunny. That's an idea.

McGeelish. Too much of a risk for the one chosen.

Horawn. Better one be one — less likely to be noticed.

Bunny. We'd not only be noticed — we'd be photographed !

McGeelish. Together then.

Chatastray. Together it is !   Come on !   [*They go at a slow march towards the porch door, Chatastray at their head ;   as they almost get there, they halt, and those following Chatastray slide backwards to where they were.   Chatastray looks around, sees they've gone back, and turns to face them.*]   What's up — aren't yous comin' ?

Bunny. Why not decide on a kinda go-between ?

McGeelish. What d'ye mean, go-between ?

Bunny. Half of us go on th' March an' half of us go to th' Memorial Service ;   it would confuse th' watchers in th' rye ;   no one could say th' writers, actors, an' poets weren't at either, an' it would be easy for us to say we were at both ?

McGeelish. That's a damn good idea.   I'm willing to go on th' March.

McGeera [*indignantly*].   You would !   All th' reporters would view you struttin' along weighed down with th' yella an' white rosette in your coat.

Horawn. An' maybe a similar cockade in his cap.

Bunny. Now, don't start a row.

McGeera. It might be wise to come to some abridgement of our hastier decision.   If we stop outa th' March, it would be wiser to ignore th' Memorial Service.   If we done both, there would be cause for a double resentment.   Afther all, Lionel Robartes won't mind now, one way or th' other.

Chatastray [*who has been leaning wearily against the gateway*]. Aw, for God's sake do something !

Bunny. Give them time, man.

Beoman [*mockingly — to Chatastray*]. Time, gentlemen, please.

Basawn [*fiercely — to Beoman*]. Can't yeh shut your mouth ! Why th' hell are yeh interferin' in Catholic affairs ?

Bunny. It would be betther for one half to go to one an' half to th' other.

Horawn. Yes, for one to take all th' risk an' th' other half to take all th' glory !
  [*Reena Kilternan rushes in ; she is a little out of breath. She is wearing a yellow and white ribbon-rosette in her blouse.*

Reena. I thought I'd be late ! Why aren't yous in ?

Horawn [*with a gesture for silence — to the girl*]. Don't interrupt — we're considering th' whole question.

Chatastray [*still leaning wearily by the gateway*]. Make a decision. For God's sake, thry to pull yourselves together.

McGeelish. It's difficult. Th' one safe way is to keep away from th' Memorial Service an' go to th' March.

Beoman. March on ! March on ! All hearts resolved on victory or death !

McGeera [*angrily — to Chatastray*]. Will yeh, for Mike's sake, make that fella o' yours keep his mouth shut !

Chatastray [*just as angrily*]. Dammit, McGeera, he's doin' what we're all afraid to do — speak our mind !

Basawn [*angrily*]. It's your bounden duty to keep from settin' a foot inside a heretical church ; and it's your duty, too, to march in any demonsthration agen Atheistic Communism !   [*To Beoman — fiercely*] An' you keep outa this ; this is our Catholic business !

Beoman. Anything happenin' in Ireland is every Irishman's business.

Reena. Th' man is right : we can't live our lives disputin' whether what we think o' doin' is right or wrong ; we have to risk a risk at times.   Come on !

Beoman [*enthusiastically*]. Thou art not conquered yet, dear land !

Bunny [*suddenly and eagerly as the Verger appears at the porch entrance*]. Couldn't we ask th' Sexton to let us slip in be th' gateway, flit along to th' grave, with no one th' wiser ?

Verger. Are youse comin' in till I shut th' door ?

McGeera [*going over to him*]. Could you let us in be the gateway to go to th' grave ? We don't wish to be too conspicuous. We're Catholics, and aren't allowed to join in any Service other than our own.

Verger [*seeming to be surprised — after a pause*]. It isn't usual, y'know. [*After another pause.*] Oh, all right — I'll open it for youse. [*He goes to the gateway, and unlocks it.*] There youse are, but why did youse come at all ?

> [*There's no answer, so he returns to the porch.*

Reena [*to the Verger*]. They sparkled the papers with their praises of him ; told stories of his help for young playwrights, actors, an' all ; so why shouldn't they come ?

[*To the others*] If youse want to respect Robartes, pull yourselves together an' do it decently.

Chatastray [*opening the gate to go in*]. Come on, lads, down to where th' grave is.

Beoman [*murmuring*]. All along, down along, all along lea.

Chatastray. Are youse comin' or not ?
    [*They all, except Reena, move slowly to the gate, crowding round it, but halting on the threshold.   A pause.*

Beoman. Go on, go on, an' don't stand there jittherin' at th' gateway !

McGeelish. I dunno ; I really don't know.

McGeera. No, nor me, either.

Reena. I do, an' so should you. [*Gesturing to the porch*] I'm goin' this way.

Basawn [*loudly*]. Why th' hell are yeh wearin' that yellow and white rosette in your blouse, if you think like that !

Chatastray [*impatiently*]. Am I to close th' gate or what ?

Bunny. Close it, close it ; give's time to think.
                                    [*Chatastray shuts it.*

Basawn [*over to the group*]. Youse are Catholics, an' mustn't go agen th' Church. [*Kneeling up on the bench to face the group*] To go to a Protestant grave would be a grave sin, mind youse, a grave sin !

McGeera. Don't mind that lout ! [*To Chatastray*] Open th' gate.

Beoman. Open th' gate and let us through. Is it to be a don't or a do ? Open th' gate an' let us through !

All [*in unison*]. Open th' gate an' let us through !

Chatastray [*opening the gate*]. Ah, sure, I never doubted you, said Rory of th' hill.
> [*The group sway inwards from the gate, sway outwards again, sway in, and sway out again ; as they sway, Kornavaun rushes in.*

Kornavaun [*excitedly and warningly*]. Hold it, boys ; hold it ! I rang up th' Archbishop's Palace : he says any joinin' in of this Service would be a grave sin, an' it's forbidden.

McGeera. We're goin' only as far as th' churchyard.

Kornavaun. That's forbidden, too, th' Palace says so.

Basawn [*excitedly*]. The Church speakin' ! Obedience !

Reena [*excitedly*]. I'm goin' inta th' church for one.
> [*She stalks to the porch, and goes into the church.*

Basawn [*looking after the girl — viciously*]. Th' ignorant little, disobedient little bitch !

Beoman. I'm goin' after you, me gallus lass.
> [*He follows her.*
> [*The 'Dead March' in Saul has been playing during the last few words spoken, and the church bell has begun to toll, a pause between each sounding. The Verger shuts the porch door, and the funeral march is then but faintly heard, the bell still tolling. The group stand silent, their heads hanging.*

Kornavaun. Pull yourselves together ! Get away from that gate, and forget it, boys. We've got to get ready for the Protest March.
> [*A mutter of women's voices is heard outside, then Angela*

and Lizzie come staggering in, hardly able to keep their feet ; they are arm in arm, supporting each other.

Lizzie. Take a holt o' yoursel, willya ! Don't go noseyin' here an' noseyin' there.

Angela. No, no noseyin'. Jus' sip sip sip.

Lizzie. Yis ; ordher o' th' day — sip be sip, be sip.
  [*As they come in front of the group watching them, they collapse and fall, stretching out side by side on the ground. Lizzie makes one or two feeble efforts to rise, gives it up, and lies prone. A pause.*

Lizzie [*beseechingly*]. For Jasus' sake, Angela, thry to pull yourself together.

END OF SCENE I

SCENE II

BEHIND THE GREEN CURTAINS

Senator Chatastray's sitting-room in his house in the town of Ballybeedhust, a little way from the town.

It is a large room, tidy, safely furnished with comfortable armchairs and settee ; a mahogany table on which stands a photograph of Chatastray himself, flanked by a vase in which no flowers stand. Two oblong windows at the back give a picture of a few trees, behind which are the tops of a few distant houses and the spire of a church ; in the centre of one window is a panel of coloured glass, circular, with a green circling frame of glass, within which is a black face of a clock having golden hands. The opposite window has a white glass diamond-shaped panel framed in ' St. Patrick's Blue ', with his red cross traversing the whole panel. The drapes, now pulled back, of the windows are of vivid green. The walls are painted soberly ; a deep brown on the back wall, a grey colour on the walls on either side. Between the windows is a small sideboard topped with glasses. A bright fire is burning to the right, semi-circled by the settee and the chairs. The door to the left is painted green, a little less vivid than the green of the drapes. Over the sideboard is a framed Abbey Theatre poster, the title shown being that of ' The Drifting Tide '. Over the mantelpiece is a bookcase filled with books, all in Gaelic. A few Paul Henry landscapes of white-washed cottages, bog of brown in middle distance, white-yellow road (bohereen), a few clumps of grass and heather, with the distant blue hills of holy Ireland overlooking and overlording all ; and a holy picture of some saint or other to keep Paul Henry company. A carpet of ordinary pattern covers the floor, and a rug stretches itself before the fireplace.

*There is no one in the room when we first see it. After a few
moments the door opens, the maid, Noneen, comes in, holds the
door open for Wycherley McGeera, a dramatist, Leslie Horawn,
a poet, Bunny Conneen, an actor, and Jack McGeelish, the gossip
writer.*

Noneen. Sit down where yous like, an' I'll tell Mr.
Chatastray you're here.

 [*They choose their seats, except McGeelish, who wanders
 about the room, poking his nose into places.*

McGeelish [*glancing at books over the mantelshelf*]. All in
Irish. [*He takes one down.*] Clean as a new pin. Never
read a damned one o' them, I'll bet. Doesn't know
more'n couple o' words.

Horawn. Do you ?

McGeelish. No, but I don't go bellowing about that it
must come back.

McGeera. Of course not. You bellow about higher things
in your gabby-scabby gossip columns.

McGeelish. More interesting than Ó Horawn's pansy
poems or your blank plays.

Bunny. Oh, quit this blastin' of each other. How're
we goin' to stand up against all that's facin' us, if we
go on in this way ? Remember how we shamed ourselves at Robartes' Memorial Service ? Be buyin'
books, Chatastray helps you fellas, doesn't he ?

Horawn. How th' hell does he ? We don't write in
Irish, an' he hasn't a damned book in English in th'
house — bar his prayer book, maybe.

McGeera. An' that's half in Latin which he doesn't know
either.

 B.G.C.—C

Horawn. An' McGeelish thinks his gossip-column a more exalted thing than my poems or your plays, McGeera ! It is, if a dusty clod of dung-soil'd grass be more exalted than a ferny wood where violets are ; or th' crimson-berried wake robin ; or th' sex symbol growing beside th' Unicorn chained to th' Pomegranate tree on th' tapestry hanging in th' Cloisters of New York.

McGeelish. Ah, for God's sake, Ó Horawn, don't be everlastin' bangling your poetic brows with home-made bayleaves !

Bunny. Looka, I didn' come here to listen to yous spittin' scorn over each other. I'm thryin' to get into th' part of Barney Ó Hay I am to play in next Abbey production, an' tho' I can't add to me reputation, I have to keep it up.

McGeera. Jasus ! What reputation ?

Bunny. As a great Abbey acthor. Oney last week, in th' *Dublin Presto* Linal Sarrosel said I was th' greatest acthor in his livin' memory, an artist of a wide fame.

McGeelish. A world-wide one from Abbey Theatre to Mooney's pub !

Horawn. All actors of th' Abbey Theatre are famous or great or world-known, or highly distinguished, known th' world over.

McGeelish [*who has been roving around poking his nose in every corner ; he is now by the sideboard, looking down at a lower drawer*]. A key sticking in it. Wonder what's there. [*He whips the drawer open.*] A buk. [*He takes it out, looks at title.*] Renan's *Life of Jesus.* Some cod book o' devotions. Who was Renan, now ?

Horawn. A one you wouldn't like to meet here or here-
after. A Breton, educated for th' priesthood, took
minor orders, flung them off him, and became an un-
believer. Mind th' book doesn't scorch your fingers !
Any other dreadful secret there ?

McGeelish [*taking a photograph from the drawer — shocked*]. A
photo of a nude !

The Rest [*in one voice*]. Show !
[*They all have a hurried look at it.*]

McGeera [*with approval*]. A handsome piece, that one, who-
ever she is.

Horawn. Do any of us know her ? [*Chorus of ' No 's.*]
Some English whore or other.

McGeelish. It isn't Noneen, anyway. That's the pious-
goin' Chatastray for you ! God Almighty, who'd ha'
thought it !

Bunny. A slim piece. Chatastray has a damned cute
eye for a girl.

McGeelish. Youse are takin' th' scandal lyin' down.
What are we goin' to do about it ? [*He has kept the
photo and has continued to stare at it while he talks.*] God,
what a revelation ! A leader of piety and upright
conduct, and now, look at this !

McGeera. Divil a one's gettin' a chance to look at it
except yourself. If Chatastray saw th' model in real
life, then, bedammit, I envy him !

McGeelish. As practisin' Catholics, youse make me sick.
Renan th' atheist and this nude girl. Oh, well, they
go together ! What's happenin' to us at all ! [*Re-
bukingly*] It's no funny thing, I can tell yous.

Horawn [*exasperated*]. Oh, for God's sake, don't be such a hypocrite ! Didn't I see you meself at pantomime and revue with your eyes out on sticks thrying to get a closer look at the ladies' legs going in and coming out of th' frills !

Bunny. Put the damned thing back, an' shut th' drawer — he may be here any minute.

McGeera. If you'd kept your probing eyes shut and your prying paws in your pockets, we'd ha' known nothin'. You've no right to be poachin' on another man's privacy. Put th' photo back and shut th' drawer.

Bunny. Is there anything else in it ?

McGeelish [*excited — rummaging a little*]. Oh God, there's more o' them at th' bottom o' th' drawer !

Horawn. Put it back ! An' remember, we've seen nothing.

McGeelish [*putting the picture back and shutting the drawer*]. It's bound to leak out one day, sometime.

McGeera. Let it, so long's it's not be us. Now sit down, and stop your Nazi searching.
        [*McGeelish sits down, trying to look unconcerned.*

Horawn [*after some moments of silence*]. Let us forget McGeelish ever found a thing.

McGeelish. All th' same, considerin', Chatastray's not a fit one to be joined with what we want to do.

McGeera. Parnell wasn't fit either ; we thrust him aside, and God made us pay a big price for our foolishness.
        [*The door is opened, and Chatastray comes briskly into the room. He greets those there.*

Chatastray. Hello, lads. Sorry for delay. Busy at th'
phone. Trouble at th' factory. [*At the sideboard.*] I
daresay none o' youse'll scorn a drink. [*Opens a
drawer filled with bottles, and lifts one out.*] Oh, these
religions ! Factory girls threaten to come out, if my
Protestant engineer marries a Catholic forewoman !
[*A knock is heard.*] Come in.

Noneen [*opens door and stands there*]. That fella, Christy
Kornavaun, is here again, an' wants to see you, urgent.

Chatastray [*explosively*]. Blast that Kornavaun and his
urgent !

McGeera [*jumping from his chair — nervously*]. If that fella
invades us here, and hears anything, he'll twist it to
mean something that never came into our minds.

Horawn. We'll just have to confine our talk to Lazarus
and Lourdes.

Chatastray [*to Noneen*]. Where is he ?

Noneen. In the hall. I left him fingering the china in th'
cabinet.

Chatastray. Prying and probing. Ireland's full of squinting probers ! [*To Noneen*] Keep him there — no, wait.
[*To the others*] Come with me to my office ; we can wait
there till Noneen gets rid of him. [*He puts bottles back
into sliding drawer and closes it.*] Quick, come on.
[*First to Noneen*] Go down and tell him I'm at a business
conference. Go on !

McGeera [*as they hurry out*]. We daren't say a word of
value with that bastard about !
                    [*They all huddle and hurry out.*

Chatastray [*to Noneen*]. Get rid of him quick as you can, Noneen.

> [*Noneen hurries out. He looks around the room, straightens a cushion on a chair. Sees the key in the sideboard drawer ; runs over, takes it out, and puts it in a pocket, then goes out.*

> [*Within a few moments the door opens rather suddenly, and Christy Kornavaun comes in hastily and rather aggressively, followed by a protesting Noneen. He is dressed in a brown suit, black wide-brimmed hat, and a flowing black tie wider and longer than the one worn by Yeats in his teenage.*

Noneen. I tell you he's at a conference, an' can't see anyone.

Kornavaun. He'll see me, so he will. Just now, I'm here for the Irish Catholic Journal, *The Catholic Buzzer*, which requests him to reply to a questionnaire giving his comments on the Cardinal Mindszenty Protest Meeting next week. So tell him that, young lady.

Noneen. He's too busy. Some other time, he said. Don't bother me now, he said.

Kornavaun. Go an' ask him again. It's urgent, tell him.
[*Noneen goes out again. Kornavaun saunters about the room. Murmuringly*] Snug as a bug in a rug here, with a saucy girl to keep him company, an' no one to watch him. [*He looks at windows.*] A clock an' a cross. Umm ; servin' God an' man. Huh. His lookin'll wear away th' clock before it'll wear away th' cross. [*He looks at the books over the mantelpiece.*] Huh ; all for show. Doesn't read a damned one o' them. Can't. God, th' whole counthry's a hothouse of humbugs.

Noneen [*coming in again*]. It's no use, he says. Important American thrade representative with him to settle big ordher. Dollars, he says. He must be private, he says.

Kornavaun. American ! A skirt, more likely.

Noneen. You'd betther ask him yourself.

Kornavaun [*leering at her*]. Maybe, now, you yourself is the private visitor.

Noneen [*vehemently*]. Sayin' that, an' you Prefect of a Sodality ! You have a dirty mind.

Kornavaun. What else would you say ? All correct an' cautiously coy while th' daylight's here to see things ; but when darkness hides things, an' th' flimsy frills of night are worn, behind green curtains th' handling sport begins. You'd be a thrill in anyone's arms. You're damned pretty before, behind, an' below, as I seen when I folleyed you upstairs.

Noneen. Mr. Chatasthray told me to give you a dhrink before you go ; an' while I'm gettin' it, I'd thank you to mind your own affairs. Mine is me own, I'd have you know.
    [*She goes to the sideboard, and takes a bottle out and a glass.*

Kornavaun. Don't be so sure, me lass. The town doesn't like you livin' alone with an unmarried man ; an' neither does the clergy either.

Noneen. I'm here with the permission of me father an' mother, an' they know more about me than the damned town, or even the clergy. Whatja want — gin or whiskey ?

Kornavaun. A tot o' whiskey with a lot o' wather. [*He goes over to her, places an arm round her waist.*] I'll wait till old Chatasthray's ready ; wait with you here, pretty one, eh ?

Noneen [*roughly and hastily removing his arm*]. You'll go when you've had your drink.   You aren't wanted here ; he told me to get rid of you. [*As he tries to put his arm round her again*] Go off from me, you gabby slug !

Kornavaun [*angrily*]. What a damned hurry you're in to have your good time with Chatasthray ! [*He almost shouts*] Well, take your chance tonight to act th' little whore with him, for it may be th' last you'll get !

Noneen [*who has half-filled the glass with water, turns suddenly, and flings it into his face*].   Now be off, before th' bottle folleys th' wather !

Kornavaun [*wiping his face with his handkerchief*].   I'll get you for this, you painted doll, you ! This is what I get for warnin' you.   Wait, you just wait ! [*He grips her arm.*]   An' tell your beau that I'll see him later on ; an' tell him if he still hides, it'll be the worse for him, see ?   I'm goin' for th' moment, but, listen ; listen, you festhered lily, you'll be sorry for flushin' Ó Kornavaun's face with a sudden wather-splash, you ignorant, impudent little [*he brings his face close to hers — hissing the last two words*] arcadian tart !
> [*He stamps from the room, and is heard stamping down the stairs, followed by the bang of an angrily-closing door. The door is opened enough to let Chatastray peep into the room.   Seeing it empty, he comes in, after a few moments.*]

Chatastray. So th' lout is gone.   Did you give him th' drink ?

Noneen. Yis ; slap into his kisser because of his ugly
threatenin' talk. He warned me to go from here.

Chatastray. Maybe, Noneen, it might be better if you
did.

Noneen. An' where would I go ? Leave here, an' I'm
one of th' gang of unemployed, unless I hied off to
England.

Chatastray. There are many worse places.

Noneen. I know, but me Ma wants me to stay near her.
I'm their one child, an' she don't like to lose sight o'
me. Me Da doesn't give a damn one way or th' other.
[*Chatastray goes to the door, passes outside, and is heard
calling the rest to come up.*

Chatastray. Come on, boys — coast's clear. [*To Noneen*]
The glasses, lass. [*Those who had gone out before, now enter
slowly and, apparently, with some hesitation ; and, one by one,
take up their former places in the room.*] Let's draw th'
green curtains, an' blind some of th' squinting eyes.
[*He slowly draws the curtains, almost keeping time to the
remarks made about them.*

McGeera. Draw th' green curtains.

McGeelish. Fitly an' firmly, draw th' green curtains.

Bunny. To blunder th' eyes—

Horawn. Looking in at th' windows.   [*A pause.*

Bunny. I hope Kornavaun hasn't got wind of us bein'
here together.

McGeera. What if he has ? We had one sufficient
shaming during th' Memorial Service, slinking off

home without a word. By God, I'll not suffer meself
to have another experience like that one !

Horawn. Here's another like you, let his *Catholic Buzzer*
say what it damn well likes !

Chatastray [*to Noneen*]. Did he say why he came, Noneen ?

Noneen. He said th' *Catholic Buzzer* sent him.

McGeera. You see, the ill-omened crawleen is on the
prowl.

Chatastray. Wonder what *The Buzzer* wants with me ?

Noneen. He is to take down comments from you about
th' comin' anti-Red demonstration, how all authors
must march in th' demonstration.

Chatastray. Oh ? Anything else, Noneen ?

Noneen. Aw, he said a lot I can't remember, but one was
that you were to name for th' *Catholic Buzzer* th'
authors you select to speak from one o' th' platforms.
                    [*Some present give a long, low whistle.*

McGeelish [*anxiously*]. Anything else, Noneen ?

Noneen. Wanted to know why Mr. Chatastray kept
friendly with them as had been condemned by *The
Buzzer*, afther havin' their books banned.

Horawn. Everything a man, anyway prominent, says if
he dares to have a thought of his own, is given a slant
by this *Catholic Buzzer* to make it appear to be sympa-
thetic to th' Reds or giving hope and courage to anti-
clerical feeling.

Bunny. Youse have got to watch your steps.

Horawn. He'll have very different hearts and minds to face this time, th' bastard !

McGeera. I'll outface him while th' moon is here an' when th' moon is gone.

Bunny. I too.

McGeelish. Another of us here.

Chatastray. So shall we all.

Horawn [*a little declamatory*]. Not yet made weak be time or fate, but sthrong in will to strive, to seek, to find, and not to yield !

Noneen. Oh, yes, an' he said, goin' out, that you must sign a great paper, Manifesto, he called it. Youse are all to sign it. The paper, already a mile long against the Reds, says more'n fifty painters of th' Royal Hibernian Academy has signed it, the Judges, th' dandy dons of th' Colleges here, Cork, an' Galway, with a few names from Belfast.

McGeera. I might sign that, but I'll not march.

Noneen. The judges will be marchin' in wigs an' gown, th' scholars in their robes. Youse, th' writers, headed be th' Irish Academy o' Letters, will folley th' Legion of Mary, with th' Band of The Catholic Boys' Brigade between youse.

Horawn. What, us ?

Bunny. With the banner inscribed ' Free Thought in a Free World ' !

McGeelish. What are we goin' to do ?

Noneen. He says th' Bishops'll lead th' March, then th' Confraternities, th' Legion of Mary, then youse.

Horawn. Then us — my God! Legion o' Mary, then us!

Noneen. Youse 'ill all look high an' mighty if th' day is fine. [*A silent pause.*] I wouldn't let meself be ordhered or led be such a one as Kornavaun.

Bunny [*rising firmly*]. Noneen's right. We must face him, an' tell him each face to his face, that we won't be there.

The Rest [*in chorus*]. Yes, let's! We vow it!
> [*A peal of thunder is heard, a slow rumble, with a sullen threat in it. They suddenly become stiff and still; the rumble gradually developing into, or changing into, the doorbell ringing clear and loud and demanding. They are all standing stiffer now, and there's a long silent pause.*]

Chatastray [*breaking the silence*]. Well, if it's Kornavaun, shall we face it out?

> [*Another silent pause.*]

McGeelish. We're not quite ready yet. We must talk th' whole thing over first.

McGeera. McGeelish is right — we have to talk it over.

Chatastray [*to Noneen, while the rest stand stiff, each with glass in hand*]. Run down, lass, and if it's Kornavaun, set him down in the hall, run up to tell us, and we can slide into th' office again. All of you bring your drinks with you.
> [*He puts bottles back in sideboard drawer, and shuts it.*

[*Noneen hurries away.   The rest stay standing, Chatastray humming a tune, very softly* — ' *Let Me Like a Soldier Fall* '.

Bunny [*doubtfully and murmuringly*]. Might be better to face him, and tell him what we think.

McGeelish [*angrily*]. You think that, do you ?   When he added to what he had heard, we'd have th' Catholic young men and Legion of Mary dhrivin' us like black cattle outa th' town.

Bunny. Aw, it wouldn't be as bad as that.

McGeera [*angrily*]. Wouldn't it, now !   For Christ's sake keep silent, if you can't find something sensible to say ! [*Noneen runs in a little out of breath from the stairs.*

Noneen. 'Tisn't him !   [*To Chatastray*] It's Beoman, th' Foreman engineer from th' factory.
[*As she ends speaking, Beoman comes into the room.   His rough but good-looking face wears a troubled look, but he has a self-contained, confident air about him, as most sure and clever workmen have.   He is dressed in brown dungarees, wears no cap, but his brown, bushy hair is a fair protection.*

Beoman. 'Scuse me, but me errand here's urgent, and sooner you know, th' betther.

Chatastray. What's wrong now ?   Have things got more serious ?

Beoman. Ay, damned serious.   [*Looking at the others present*] Can I speak out ?

Chatastray. Friends here.   All artists, Martin, who put no pass on us poor business fellas.

Beoman. It's well for them. It's all about the Sally Timahoe and Jimmy Coulter affair.

Chatastray [*a little impatient*]. I guessed that ; well, go on.

Beoman. I'd rather wait till th' others come ; they're sendin' a deputation here, — two girrls, an' it wouldn't be fair to speak before they come.

Chatastray. Oh, Lord ! [*To Beoman*] All right. Sit down, Martin. [*Martin finds a place to sit ; the others follow suit, so does Chatastray with a long sigh.*] Where were we, lads, when we broke off ?

McGeera. About facing Kornavaun and what we are determined to do.

Chatastray. Well, we've decided to face out Kornavaun — one ; and — two, refuse to take part in th' Demonstration.

Bunny. We've decided to do these things, but we haven't yet planned out a way o' doin' them.

Beoman. Kornavaun — that was th' guy that was talkin' to th' girrls in th' factory.

Chatastray. Oh ? What th' hell was he doin' there ?

Beoman. Blathered to th' girrls about bein' firm, an' that a Catholic girrl marryin' a Protestant wasn' a marriage at all ; upset them all, an' held up th' work. I hooked him, and bid him a rough goodbye at th' factory gate.

McGeelish [*indignantly*]. You had no right to interfere with him. He was only doin' his duty as a good Catholic.

Beoman. Oh ? Well, he was interferin' with two of my workers, an' I don't give a bouquet to anyone meddlin' in our factory affairs.

Chatastray. I've got more of those postcards for you, Martin. [*He goes to the sideboard, unlocks the drawer, and takes a number of picture-postcards from it. He brings them to Beoman.*] There you are : Cézanne, Corot, an' Renoir, with one of Goya's, *The Maja.* Watch out for anyone who sees it with you. [*To the rest*] Martin, here, is thryin' to get to know something of the great artists.

Beoman. Oh, thanks, Mr. Chatastray. Wish I could go to London like you. I will one day to see all of these.

Chatastray. You won't see half of them there. The lovely naked lady is in Madrid.

Horawn [*impatiently*]. For God's sake, Chatastray, let's keep to the problem before us all.
    [*Beoman glances at the pictures, and then puts them in a pocket.*

McGeelish. We ought to take into account all that happened to pretty Reena Kilternan afther she'd ventured to be at th' Robartes' Memorial..

Bunny. Nothin' happened for a few weeks, an' proud she was she'd gone ; but afther a month, th' paper she sent occasional articles to suddenly found they needed her no more. Now they hardly speak to her at Legion of Mary meetin's. [*A pause*] Good thing she had her job as an hospital nurse.

Chatastray. We should ha' gone with her, but never mind now about Reena Kilternan. We won't march — that's settled.

Bunny [*hesitantly*]. No, no, of course not.

Horawn. Our place is in no rabblement, no crowd,

senses blurred be blarin' bands, even when it's led be a smaller rabble of mitred bishops.

McGeelish [*enthusiastically*]. You're damn right !

Horawn [*getting excited — standing up*]. Th' writer's place is th' cool contentment of quiet, in a corner where no voice comes ; no car drives by ; no child's laugh disturbs ; no touch from a woman to ruffle th' still-ness of thought ; only birdsong and th' gentle ripple of a rose on its own bush.

Beoman. Away from life.

McGeera [*angrily — to Beoman*]. Oh, shut up, you ! What d'ye know about th' needs of artists ?

Horawn [*relaxing a little*]. No rabblement for us — sacred or profane. We're above them, some of us even members of th' Irish Academy of Letters.

McGeera [*impatiently*]. Aw, come off it, Horawn, balloonin' your little distinction of bein' an Academician of Irish Letthers !

Horawn [*annoyed — coldly*]. It must be more'n a little dis-tinction, or you wouldn't be damagin' people's ears with your cries for help to be elected.

McGeera [*rising out of his chair — angrily*]. That's a damned lie ! I care as much about your Academy as I do about th' first spit from me mouth first time in th' mornin' !

McGeelish [*mockingly*]. Th' laurelled heads of your Academy are each laurelled be all the others !

Horawn. When th' two of youse reach th' level of quality required, youse'll be elected : at present, thank God, we've no place for scribblers.

McGeelish. Remember what the critic, Jim Gasper, said of your work, Horawn ? That your poethry never felt th' earth ; it dangled over it, slid down towards th' ground, glided up from it ; never goin' far up, never touchin' down.

McGeera. Thank God, I'm not an Academician !

Horawn. How fortunate, for you were almost made one at our last meetin'.

McGeera [*staggered*]. Who — me ?

Horawn. Ay, you : you were beaten but by one vote.

McGeera [*mollified and flattered*]. Well, that was damned decent of the Academicians.

Horawn. Now that I know your feelings about it, I'll make sure your name doesn't come before us again.

McGeera [*fluttered and anxious*]. Oh, don't let a few hot an' hasty words put you out. After all, an Academy founded by Yeats carries an honour to its members. I can honestly say I deserve a place there.

McGeelish [*maliciously*]. Then you're the only one who can.

McGeera [*indignantly*]. Well, I'm something other than a hack journalist an' scurvy gossip-writer.

McGeelish. Meanin' me ? Maybe you don't know that th' one vote that did you in was cast be Horawn himself.

Horawn [*hastily — to McGeera*]. McGeelish doesn't know, couldn't know, how th' votin' went.

B.G.C.—D

McGeelish. Ay, an' gave his reason, too, that your plays weren't worth even th' honour of a common school performance.

Horawn [*enraged*]. Jasus, you are a malicious bastard, McGeelish !

McGeelish [*springing to his feet and making a step towards Horawn, but held back by Chatastray*]. I'll let no guy call me a bastard !

Chatastray [*remonstrating*]. This is no time for youse to go fighting together !

Beoman. Or place either, in th' quiet land of Erin.
   [*As they struggle, a loud, long ring of the doorbell is heard. They all jump from their chairs (except Beoman).*

All [*together — except Beoman*]. Kornavaun !
   [*They grab their glasses and make towards the door just as it opens and Noneen appears there.*

Noneen [*to Chatastray*]. A young lady, sir, from th' Legion of Mary, to see you.

Chatastray [*with a groan*]. Oh, Lord !
   [*The others get into their chairs again, and settle themselves there.*
   [*Reena Kilternan enters the room. This attractive young dame is dressed in a tailored suit and nylons and black shoes. The whole appearance is a little austere and sober, but a gay-coloured scarf around her neck pays a tribute to youth and loveliness. She wears no hat, and carries a small suitcase.*

Reena. Good evenin', gentlemen. [*She glances at the green curtains.*] How nice th' curtains are ! What great thought and high ideas go floatin' round here behind these lovely green curtains !

Beoman. Aw, for God's sake, lady !

Reena [*looking for a moment at Beoman in a surprised way, but deciding not to notice the remark*]. It's nice to have caught you all together just as Mr. Kornavaun said.

Chatastray. What d' ye mean — jus' as Kornavaun said ?

Reena. He came to th' Legion of Mary office to tell us you were havin' a meetin' here, addin' something I didn't believe an' don't believe — that youse were wobblin', an' I should hurry here to hook youse into rememberin' what we all have to do.

Bunny. A meetin' ?

McGeera. Wobblin' ?

McGeelish. Hook us ?

Reena [*shyly*]. I'm a nurse, but I've tried my hand at writing a short story or two, but I got only a few accepted. [*Resignedly*] Never mind ! It's lovely to come here, an' meet th' leaders of Ireland's thought.

Beoman [*sardonically*]. You've come to th' wrong place, lady. Leaders of thought are elsewhere an' far away.

Reena [*somewhat puzzled*]. Eh ? This is a proper place, sir, where th' writers come together ; always brave, but will be braver from the grace given through the sacred Demonstration ; braver than ever leading us all into th', into th', th'——

Beoman [*ejaculatory*]. Desert !

Reena. Pasture, sir, of wholesome, pure, and decent thought in poem, novel, an' play.

Beoman. Oh, my God !

Reena. Yes, sir ; as Dr. Farren, Bishop of Derry, said, it is filthy literature that corrupts Irishmen and makes them ripe for Communism.

Beoman. Th' Bible, you know, can be pretty bad, miss.

Reena [*puzzled — to the others*]. I don't know what he means, but this is no time for discussion : we have work to do. [*She gives all her attention to the others.*] All Ireland'll be there ; first th' Bishops an' clergy, secular an' ordhers, then the Ministhers of th' State, then the Law. Youse will folley th' Legion of Mary marchin' in front of your banner, a blazin' torch over the motto, Free Thought in a Free World, headed be the band of th' Boys' Brigade. We'll arouse Europe an' America, an' Communism'll get a vital set-back. For being naughty, I've lost me honorary job as an organiser, and [*gayly*] have to do the donkey work now. So I have your insignia here with me.

[*She opens up her suitcase.*

Chatastray [*embarrassed*]. Insignia ? What kinda insignia ?
[*She takes a wide sash of yellow and white from the suit-case, and goes to Chatastray.*

Reena. You're to lead your contingent, so you wear a sash and a rosette. Stand up. [*He does so.*] Bend your head a little. [*He does so meekly.*] Rosettes for th' others. [*She drapes it over the right shoulder and arranges it across his breast, then stands back to admire him.*] Now you look lovely. Now a rosette.

[*She pins one to his left shoulder.*

Beoman. An' feels that way, too.

Reena [*presenting a white and yellow beribboned rosette to each of the others*]. Please put them into your coats now. [*She goes to Beoman, and offers him one.*] For you, friend.

Beoman [*rather reluctantly*]. Sorry to disappoint such a pretty lady, miss, but I won't be marching.

Reena [*with sure confidence*]. Oh, but you will ; you simply must march.

Bunny. He's a Protestant, an' doesn't hold with us.

Reena. Of course, he holds with us ! This isn't a march of one creed agen another, but a march of all Christian creeds agen th' Reds.

Beoman. Yes, miss, agen me. You see, I happen to be a Red.

Reena [*shocked*]. You aren't ; you couldn't be — not in Ireland !

Beoman. For years, pretty lady, for years.

Reena. What, with th' devils who persecute th' Church, deny God, and put our priests to silence ?

Beoman. An' th' world not a ha'porth th' worse for their silence. You see, young lady, they must. submit to the laws of the land they live in ; where they move an' have their being. They must be subject to the State, without any cod benefit or privilege of priesthood.

Reena [*turning to the others*]. What is this fella doin' here, among good an' honest Catholics ? [*To Beoman*] You have no right to such opinions in this holy land of ours.

Beoman. Mine as much as yours, lady, and remember your motto — Free Thought in a Free World.

Reena [*taken aback somewhat — turning to the others still fiddling with their rosettes*]. Oh, put them safely in your coats, please, and don't be twisting them about as if you were half afraid of them. [*They begin to do this rather sheepishly.*] It's a shame you don't try to help this odd man hiding from God, heedless of his spiritual state, a far wanderer from the help of our Blessed Lady, God help him.

Beoman [*going over to her, taking her gently by the arm*]. Well, thanks, pretty lady, for taking my fierce opinions so softly.
    [*She turns as if to repulse him angrily, hesitates, looks into his eyes, and suddenly pats him sympathetically and gently on the arm. He goes back to his place.*
    [*A loud ring of the doorbell, causing the authors to half start from their seats again. They are all now finely festooned with their rosettes.*
    [*A few moments later Noneen appears at the door.*

Noneen. Th' deputation, sir, and that other fella with them.

Chatastray. What other fella?

Reena. Mr. Kornavaun probably; he told me he was to lead the girls.

Beoman. I can guess where he'd like to lead them to.
    [*The deputation of three girls, two young, one about 36, led by Kornavaun, enter the room. He is wearing a yellow and white sash, similar to that worn by Chatastray. The girls all wear rosettes, so all there are now decorated with the exception of Beoman.*

Older Girl [*stepping forward a little*]. We're all ready to come out, Mr. Chatastray, unless you act by stoppin' Jim Coulter, the Protestant, marrying Sally Timahoe, a Catholic girl.

Chatastray. I can't interfere, Mary; th' law allows him to marry anyone he chooses.

Kornavaun [*stepping out to stand beside the girl*]. Man's fallible law, Mr. Chatastray. We're here, not to honour or defend that law, but to defend and honour th' law of th' Church.

Chatastray [*to the girl, ignoring Kornavaun*]. I hope you realise what a stoppage means, Mary? We have important American orders in hand ; if the factory stops, even for a few days, these orders can't be delivered in time. The order'll be lost, with others to follow, and th' factory'll have had a dream that didn't come true.

Kornavaun. Th' Faith is of more importance than any, or many, American dollars.

Younger Girl. Looka, if she doesn't break from him, or he doesn't break from her, we go out, and stay out till either him or her give over th' idea of living together — for what they'll call a marriage won't be one ; or till both of them flit from th' factory.

Chatastray. An' where'm I goin' to get a forewoman like Timahoe or a machinist like Coulter? Some of our machines are wobbling, and Coulter keeps them moving. Th' American ordher, if we finish it, will give a chance to us to get better machines, and so make th' factory more productive. In heaven's name, think of what you're doin' !

Kornavaun. You can't get away with that blather, Chatastray. Th' Church condemns any Catholic girl that marries an atheist, or even a believin' Protestant, so it is your bounden duty to oppose this union. You must stand be th' Church.

Chatastray. I stand be th' law, Kornavaun, and, even if I would, I can't prevent these two from joining themselves together.

Kornavaun. You can try.

Chatastray. No, Kornavaun ; I won't even try to do it.

Older Girl. Well, girls, out we come ! Come on ; we're wastin' time.
[*The three women go out. They are hardly out before a cry is heard from Noneen. Chatastray starts towards the door, but before he gets there, two men with handkerchiefs over the lower parts of their faces, and with short stout sticks in their right hands, appear in the doorway, and one of them shuts it with a bang.*

Noneen [*crying loudly outside*]. Mr. Chatastray, stop them ; help me, help !

1st Man [*pushing Chatastray roughly back from the doorway*]. Get back, you !

Chatastray. What is happening to me maid ?
[*Sound of a car is heard starting and moving away outside.*

2nd Man. She's been taken to be taught that this town doesn't allow a young unmarried girl to live with an unmarried man.

1st Man [*in a curious gloating way*]. Since she wouldn't listen to th' Church, she'll soon be ready to listen to us.

Reena [*disturbed*]. Oh, you shouldn't do this ; you mustn't hurt her.

1st Man. A hurt body's betther th'n a hurt soul, miss.

Beoman [*agitated — going over to face the two men standing with their backs to the door*]. Here, you two, outa th' way till I phone th' police !

2nd Man. Garda, we call them now, Beoman. We know you, an' don't take ordhers from any atheistic Communist, so take it easy ; she's a Catholic girl, and this is none o' your affair, see ?

Reena. You mustn't hurt the young girl, men. We won't let you !

2nd Man. Leave her to us, young woman ; we know what to do with her.

Beoman [*violently*]. You thugs ! [*He suddenly leaps at one of the men, whips the stick from him, and stands by the door.*] [*To the authors*] Give us a hand to hunt these bastards outa th' house ! [*No one stirs.*]   And find out what has happened to th' young lass.

[*No one stirs.*

1st Man [*quietly but triumphantly — to Beoman*]. You see, Beoman ? Not a word ; not a move outa them.

Beoman [*bitterly*]. No, not a mouse stirring !

Reena [*running to Beoman*]. I'll go !

2nd Man [*getting in front of her, and rather roughly shoving her back*]. No, you don't — not yet ! The men know the wiser thing to do.

Beoman [*going to Chatastray and catching him by the arm*]. Th' two of us will tackle them ; you go for one, I'll soon settle th' lout with th' stick !

Chatastray [*gloomily*]. It's no use, it's no use, Beoman.

McGeelish [*angrily — to Beoman*]. Are you incapable of minding your own business, man? This winding brook of ours finds its own way down hill, through cornfield and grassland, so don't let your interferin' babbling trickle away into any of its ripplin'!

McGeera. McGeelish is right — we have neither wish nor need for any promptin' from a factory hand, even if he is an engineer.

Beoman. A brook that babbles, chatters, and bends, but never reaches th' brimming river.

1st Man. Well, you see now : they not only give way to Catholic action, but like it, too. So go, friend, an' leave us to deal with our own kind.

Beoman [*after a moment's pause*]. I'll go, an' leave them to their blessed saints, Stepaslide, Touchnrun, Dubudont, an' Goslow. [*To the Two Men*] I go straight to the police.

2nd Man [*good-humouredly*]. All right, all right. Go anywhere you like so you go from here.
[*As Beoman makes for the door.*

1st Man [*calling out*]. You're forgettin' my stick, friend.

Beoman. No I'm not ; I have it here.

1st Man. Well, leave it here, please.

Beoman. Let him who has a stick come an' get it for you ; or, better still, come th' two o' youse together. [*The Two Men stay silent and still.*] Nothin' doin'. [*To the others*] You see ? Face th' thugs, an' they are silent an' stay still. Ah, th' quiet land of Erin. [*He lilts the last sentence. To Reena*] Come with me, pretty lady, to the police.

[*She makes to join him, but 1st Man puts an arm in front of her.*

1st Man. No, young lady ; as you are a Legion of Mary lass, an' should be with us, betther stay here with the rest.

Beoman [*giving 1st Man a violent and angry shove that sends him staggering against his companion ; catching Reena by the arm and pulling her to the door behind him*]. Down with you, pretty lass, an' when you're at the hall door, call up, an' I'll join you.

    [*Reena runs out while Beoman stands with his back to the door, watching the Men. After a few moments, Reena calls up to him.*

Reena [*calling up from below*]. Right here now, young man, with the hall door open !

Beoman [*as he goes out*]. Goodbye, all you ripples on a lost river.

    [*The Two Men wait a few moments, leaning, one on either side of the door. Then the sound of a car pulling up outside is heard, and they become attentive.*

    [*The door is opened, and a Third Man enters. Half his face is covered by a handkerchief — the lower half.*

3rd Man. Everything all right ? Got him ?

2nd Man. Yeah ; and we're waitin'.

3rd Man [*to the others*]. Youse sit quiet like youse are, see ? Nice an' quiet. [*To Chatastray*] You, Chatastray, come along with us — we want to have a quiet chataway with you, see ?

2nd Man [*mockingly*]. Come, birdie, come.

3rd Man [*angrily*]. Shut up, you! There must be no mockery in th' work we do for th' honour of our Blessed Lady, golden patroness of our Irish womanhood. [*To Chatastray*] Come on, you.

> [*Chatastray rises slowly, hesitates a little, then goes towards the door, one man goes before him, 2nd Man follows, then 3rd Man leaves, shuts the door, and turns a key in the lock outside. They are heard going down, followed by the sound of a car leaving below in the street, in front of the door. The others sit huddled together where they were, silent and ashamed. A pause.*

McGeelish [*raising his head to glance towards the others — with some bitterness*]. His atheist Joseph Renan won't be much of a help to him now!

Horawn [*with mocking bitterness*]. Nor your Jesus Christ neither!

END OF SCENE II

SCENE III

DAY OF THE MARCHING SOULS

The Day of the Demonstration, but there is no sign of any interest in it within the sitting-room of Dennis Chatastray. It is the same room, with a difference — it has lost its tidiness and sense of order. The chairs are still where they were left when Chatastray was carried off ; now, the table is unsightly with a dirty plate, glasses, and a cup and saucer ; a few empty bottles of beer lie on their sides under the table. On the floor, nearer the window, lie his white and yellow sash and rosette ; and an odd book and some newspapers are scattered about the floor of the room.

Although it is early daytime, the Green Curtains are still drawn, and now and again muffled sounds of life outside go across the room. One electric light serves to hide the room's dimness. The one bright place there is the fireplace where a cheerful fire is burning.

Chatastray sits sprawled in an armchair before the fire. The left sleeve of his coat has been cut off, showing a bandaged arm, another bandage is around his forehead, and a dark-blue bruise shows under his right eye. On a chair to one side of him is a gramophone on which is a record which has been, or is to be, played.

Chatastray is gazing aimlessly into the fire, a glass of sherry in his uninjured hand.

As he sits there, a band is heard playing 'Fainne Geal an Lae' — 'Fair Dawning of the Day'; but he sits motionless, aimlessly gazing into the fire-glow. As the sound of the music fades off into the distance, a knock is heard at the room door, but Chatastray takes no notice of it. After a pause, the knock is given again, a little louder than the gentle one given before.

55

Chatastray [*loudly and angrily — without turning his head*].
Go to hell !
    [*The door opens gently and slowly, and Reena Kilternan
    stands on its threshold.*

Reena. A fair goodday to you, friend.

Chatastray [*savagely*]. Aw, go to hell !

Reena [*coming into the room*]. Now, now, what's happening
    to you ? I found th' hall door wide open ; and, oh,
    look at the state th' room is in ! [*Chatastray remains
    silent.*] I brought you a message from Noneen. [*He
    stays silent.*] D'ye hear ? — from little Noneen.

Chatastray. I don't care if the door is open or shut. I
    want to be left alone ; an' I don't want to hear about
    her . . . or about anyone else.

Reena [*ignoring his remark*]. What a state everything is in !
    We must do something about it. [*She gathers the soiled
    chinaware together to carry them away.*] Your kitchen is
    on th' left, isn't it ?

Chatastray. Please go away !

Reena. Isn't it ?

Chatastray. Yes, yes.
    [*She goes out carrying the delft-ware with her, and returns
    in a few moments, straightening up the other things
    scattered about as she talks to him.*

Reena. She sent a message by me to you. [*He is silent.*]
    She said you weren't to worry about her, and that she
    was all right, and herself again. [*A pause.*] Pity you
    can't say th' same about yourself.

Chatastray. I went through a tough time.

Reena. Of course, but not so bad as Noneen's. Do you
know what they done to her ? [*He remains silent.*]
Brought her to a house where two women stripped her.

Chatastray [*quickly and bitterly*]. Legion of Mary lasses.
Plain-faced bitches too.

Reena. How did you know ?

Chatastray [*grimly*]. I guessed it.

Reena. Oh ? They were a disgrace to the Legion. Then
these kind ladies put a nightdress on her. The men,
with one o' th' women, tied her to a telegraph pole,
and there she stayed till th' morning postman set her
free.

Chatastray. Well, God was kinder than his eager defenders
— he sent no frost.

Reena. No ; he sent no frost.   [*A pause.*

Chatastray. Where is she now ?

Reena. Her father tried to persuade her to see th' clergy
to tell them how sorry she was for her — her——

Chatastray [*mockingly*]. Her sin !
[*Turning to look at her for the first time.*

Reena. That's what they call it. [*A pause.*] She got a
deep shock from it all. Since it happened, she has
drifted into an odd way of thinkin' : she hasn't a good
word for religion. It will be a time before she endures
th' name of Ireland again. It was a deep shock.

Chatastray [*sullenly and half defiantly*]. Well, so was mine.

Reena. Nonsense ! You're near as well as ever you were.
Your head an' hand will be well in less 'n a week.

Chatastray. You seem to know a helluva lot about them.

Reena. I do. I visited you several times in hospital when you were lying for th' two days there to soften th' shock.

Chatastray [*some astonishment in his tone*]. You did ?

Reena. I suppose you didn't recognise me in me uniform.

Chatastray. Uniform ? What uniform ?

Reena. A nurse. I'm on th' staff. I'm a nurse. That's th' way I earn me livin'. Didya think I had an income ?

Chatastray [*turning his gaze away to resume his stare at the fire*]. I didn't know ; I didn't care ; and I don't care now.

Reena [*quietly*]. Why should you care ?   [*A pause.*

Chatastray. Is Noneen at home ?

Reena. No.

Chatastray [*troubled*]. No ? Why not ?

Reena. She had a stiff time with her father. I've told you — wanted her to go to th' priest and beg pardon.

Chatastray [*a little surprised and doubtful*]. An' she wouldn't ?

Reena. She wouldn't, though her father threatened her with a thrashing if she didn't.

Chatastray [*violently*]. Th' damned hypocrite ! He never failed to come every week here to take away two-thirds of Noneen's wage !

Reena. Th' poor man was frightened as you were.

Chatastray. As I was ? Me ? [*Resentfully.*]

Reena. When you failed to resist when th' men came, as Beoman wanted you to do. We're all frightened — those in th' North as well as us in th' South ; th' men who took Noneen an' you . away with them were frightened of faith, and of anyone setting himself apart from th' others an' themselves ; an' you an' your friends frightened of fighting for yourselves, or for anything disliked by th' clergy and th' foggy explosion of townsfolk talk.

Chatastray. An' what th' hell does a Legion of Mary lass know about such things — tell me that ?

Reena. Some of us do a little thinking, sir. I've thought long about it these many days, an' other things too. We are a huddled nation frightened undher th' hood of fear.   [*A pause.*

Chatastray. What did — they — do — to — Noneen ?

Reena [*maliciously*]. Don't you worry about her — Noneen's all right.

Chatastray [*resentfully*]. I do worry about her, see ? She's more important to me than you are.

Reena [*a little hurt*]. I know that ; I'm of no importance to you at all.

Chatastray [*quickly*]. I didn't mean it that way, lass ; [*turning to gaze at her*] really I didn't. You are very kind to come here ; your sympathy is really very welcome — honestly ! You're pretty, too. [*A pause.*] But I want to be by meself ; just by meself.

Reena. You'll be by yourself often enough when you're old ; it's not good for you now. See how I've tidied up th' place !

B.G.C.——E

Chatastray [*turning away from looking at her*]. Oh, damn th'
place ! I'd rather you'd left it alone.

Reena. No one and nothing can be left alone in this
world. As long as you're alive, you'll have to bear
being touched by th' world you live in.

Chatastray [*sardonically*]. Be God, I've been hard touched
be th' world already. I've had enough of it.

Reena [*quietly*]. You deserved all you got.

Chatastray [*jumping from his chair, going to her, and catching
her arm, angrily*]. I want none o' your Legion o' Mary
cant, me lass ! There was nothin' wicked between me
'n' little Noneen. [*He starts to drag her towards the door.*]
Go on, get out ! You've no business here !

Reena. See, you're afraid of me, now ! [*He lets her go.*]
You got what you got through th' cowardice of your
friends and your own . . . over th' years ! I've
looked back, an' now I remember things done which
shouldn't ha' been done, but you nor your friends ever
done a thing, ever said a word against them ! No
wondher Martin Beoman laughed when I said I had
come to the leaders of Ireland's thought ! Big fellas
behind th' green curtains, but in the open a flock of
scurvy sheep ! Scant of wool an' scabby !

Chatastray [*nonplussed and ashamed*]. We had to use caution ;
we had to be prudent.

Reena [*sarcastically*]. Oh, fine ! Your caution an' prudence
has presented you with a bruised body, a troubled
mind, an' a sick soul. My God, you're a highlight of
cowardice to yourself an' us all !
   [*Chatastray has gone back to the fireplace where he stands
   dejected and limp.*]

Chatastray. Please remember that it is you in th' form of a crowd that forces us to be what we were, what we are now.

Reena. You never tried to tell us how to think, what to do, where to go. Even th' louder murmurs of Beoman frightened youse all, as, indeed, I heard meself. Youse yourselves helped to form th' crowd that cry out against youse.

Chatastray [*impatiently*]. All right, all right ; oh, let's forget it all for a while. Looka, I don't even know your name.

Reena. Oh, if you're that much interested, my name's Reena Kilternan.

Chatastray. Mine's Dennis. Have a glass o' wine with me — Reena.

Reena. Nice of you to ask me, — Dennis.
[*He fills out two wineglasses of sherry, giving one to her, the other to himself; holds his glass towards hers, she touches his, and they drink.*

Both [*together*]. Cheers.
[*Outside through some street a band is heard playing the 'Marseillaise', on its way to form up for the Demonstration. Immediately — after listening for a moment, Chatastray loses his happy look, hastily puts his glass down on the table, and turns away from Reena.*

Chatastray. God Almighty, they're marching to th' *Marseillaise* ! Th' groggy gang of hypocrites ! Cowardly minds an' spent-out lives trudge along on unsteady feet to th' rhythm of th' *Marseillaise*, without any idea of the surging revolt in its melody !

Reena. Have you ?

Chatastray. Have I what ?

Reena. Any idea of th' surging revolt in its melody ? You didn't show many signs of it facing Kornavaun an' his hooligan friends.

Chatastray [*returning to sit a little sullenly in his chair*]. That was different.   There were too many against me.

Reena. What, with your friends and warrior Beoman eager to stand out in front of th' defence ?

Chatastray. My friends wouldn't budge, as you well know.

Reena. They're valueless friends then ; indeed, dangerous ones.

Chatastray. We're not afraid to have our independent thoughts.   Many a time, straight things have been said in this very room.

Reena. I'm sure o' that : well hidden behind th' green curtains ! Th' windas shut behind th' curtains. None of th' brave thoughts, though, were let escape out into th' cool air of life. Well, let's pull th' green curtains back now, an' open th' windas.
   [*She goes to the windows, and seizes one of the drapes to pull it back.*

Chatastray [*hastily*]. Don't pull th' curtains back ! Leave them as they are ! Damn it, woman, don't be so fond of meddling !

Reena [*hesitating for a moment*]. It is day, Dennis, and each day brings a challenge. It isn't good to live an' move be candle-light when th' sun is out.
   [*She sweeps one side of the curtain back.*

Chatastray. No, don't, Reena. Miss Kilternan, don't !

Reena [*ready to pull back the second side*]. Face th' light of
day ! [*She sweeps the second part of the curtain back.*] Now
we can breathe more easily, think more freely, for th'
green curtains are folded away. Now we'll open th'
window.

Chatastray. I tell you I don't want to touch th' town
again ; don't want even to touch with my foot th'
pavement in the street outside th' door !
    [*Reena opens the window. The sky is clear and blue, the
    sun is shining ; the tramp of feet is heard, tramp of a
    crowd, in the distance.*

Reena. Let th' old air out ; let th' new air in. There's
th' tramp of people's feet, embedded in a one
resolve, marching to th' meeting.

Chatastray. I don't want to hear it. I want to shut my
eyes and my mind away from it all.

Reena. Listen, you foolish man : when you shut out th'
people, you are shutting out God. [*She goes over to him
and lays a hand gently on his shoulder.*] Come, face it ;
look out over it all. It is part of ourselves. Come
over, an' be brave. [*He rises slowly and as slowly goes over
to the window, looking out on the town. His hand steals over
to hers and closes over it as they stand side by side looking out
over the town.*] There you are ; there they go ; an
army with banners marching in th' wrong direction.

Chatastray [*surprised at her words*]. Th' wrong direction ?
I thought you believed they were on th' right road ?

Reena. I did ; I don't now. Do you ?

Chatastray [*hesitant*]. I don't really know.

Reena. I'm not asking you if you know ; I'm just asking you if you believe one way or th' other. Will you mingle th' patter of your feet with th' feet of th' marchers ; or will you sit here sullen, angry, undecided, and afraid ?

Chatastray [*resentful*]. Who th' hell d'ye think you are — my father confessor, or what ?

Reena. I'm asking if your braver thoughts are never to be more than an echo given back from — [*she gestures indicating the walls of the room*] these four walls, muffled into a cautious whisper by your gallant green curtains ?

Chatastray. Draw those green curtains again, please — th' voice carries far in the town of Ballybeedhust. Shut th' windows an'——

Reena. Th' window is open, the curtains pulled back ; if you want to hide th' world away, shut th' one an' draw th' others yourself, an' I will say goodbye.

Chatastray. Goodbye ? Well, no one asked you here. Go as soon as you like. [*Loudly — turning to face her.*] Go now !

Reena [*quietly*]. Very well, but first, let me view th' ceremonial of you shuttin' th' window an' drawin' th' green curtains close again.

Chatastray. You'd like that, wouldn't you ? But you won't see it, so go.

Reena [*taking the yellow and white sash and rosette from the table, going nearer to where he is sitting, and holding these out to him*]. Here, brave man, take these an' put them on you ; then window shut, or window open, green curtains drawn or pulled back, you will feel uncomfortable, but safe.

[*He rises from his chair, angrily snatches the sash from her hand, makes a movement as if to fling it out of the window, stops his arm in its flight, and throws the sash on to the table.*

Chatastray [*angrily*]. Leave things alone, will you !

Reena [*laughing*]. For one mad hopeful second, I thought you were goin' to throw it out of th' window.

Chatastray [*facing her*]. Looka, what brought you here ? Why did you come stealing into a place, uninvited ; maybe where you weren't wanted ?

Reena. I told you — I brought a message from Noneen.

Chatastray [*gripping her tight by both arms*]. You came as well to have a laugh at all that has happened to me.

Reena. No, not to laugh.

Chatastray. To enjoy th' feeling then at another's popular punishment.

Reena. Not that either.

Chatastray. What th' hell then ? Weren't you one of th' screeching gang thinking up evil between Noneen an' me ?

Reena. I thought so, at first, but I didn't screech th' thought. Now, let me go, please.

Chatastray [*gripping her arms still and shaking her*]. Then why did you come here ; why did you come ? — go on, answer.

Reena. I imagined you had a heart that wanted to be brave, so I came to help you.

Chatastray [*astounded and mocking*]. Jasus, she came to help me !

Reena. Noneen told me th' sort o' man you were ; that you were kind, considherate, an' that you shielded her when even her father was in one of his many dhrinkin' bouts.

Chatastray [*bitterly*]. Did she tell you them things ? Did she tell you I failed to stand in front of her when she needed shieldin' most ? I loved th' lass as her father should have done ; coaxed her into reading books and into hearing the finest of Irish folksong and the simpler music of th' greater men ; but I failed her. [*He sinks an ashamed face on Reena's shoulder.*] Oh, Reena, I failed her in the end !

Reena [*soothingly and encouragingly*]. Hush, now. You hadn't it in you to do more then. It is good for you to feel this way, Dennis. You have all th' good things in you that our Noneen spoke of to me.

Chatastray. Well, then, what lack I yet ?

Reena [*lifting his head from her shoulder to look directly into his face*]. Guts !

Chatastray [*resentfully*]. There you go again — saying a good thing, then adding a sting that takes its worth away !

Reena. Oh, stand up to things, man, unless you want to lie down undher them ? [*A pause.*] Are you content to lie down undher them ? [*He makes no attempt to answer.*] Oh, well ! [*She takes up the yellow and white ribbon sash, and offers it to him.*] Here you are.

Chatastray [*retreating away from it*]. What, that ? What for ?

Reena. Why, to wear, of course.   Your friends'll be here any minute, now, to bring you to th' starting-point of the Procession.   You were proposed last night for th' Ordher they have all joined ;   you were elected, and they bring you th' sackcloth coat, th' badge of th' Order.

Chatastray [*dismayed*]. Ordher ?   What Ordher ?

Reena. Th' Third Ordher of th' Brothers Repentant.

Chatastray [*indignantly*]. I won't join them ;   I won't wear a sackcloth jacket !

Reena [*approvingly*]. Good.   Now, will you march ?

Chatastray [*doubtfully — after a pause*]. I suppose so.

Reena. Do you want to march ?   Do you think you ought to march ?

Chatastray. I don't want to ;   I don't think I should ; but it isn't a question of either ;   it is a question of I must.   If I refused, I'd be an exile from everything.

Reena. As long as you have life, you can be exiled from nothing ;   but even if you go, you'll be forever watched, for they'll never trust you.   You'll never be able to take a step other than one in chime with theirs ; never be able to venture a thought other than one looking lovely written on a three-leaved shamrock.

Chatastray [*vehemently*]. You're right, Reena, by God !   I won't go ;   th' Brothers Repentant can go to hell in their own sweet way and their sackcloth coats !
   [*A loud insistent ring at the hall door below is heard.*

Reena. That's probably them.   Shall I go down and tell them to be off with themselves ?

Chatastray. Yes, yes, do. [*As Reena is at the door.*] No, wait a minute. [*She pauses on the threshold.*] Better let them come up, and hear what they have to say. [*Reena pauses at the door, looking doubtfully at Chatastray; then goes out to admit the visitors. He paces the room uneasily, looks out of the window, then, as he hears them at the door, he goes to the fireplace, and awaits their incoming. The writers come in — Horawn, Bunny, McGeera, McGeelish, and Kornavaun. They are wearing dun-coloured jackets of sackcloth, with a conspicuous cross of coloured cloth stitched over the breast; the shaft of each cross is yellow, the arms white within a panel of bright green. Each, too, is wearing the white and yellow rosette pinned to the left shoulder. Chatastray stares at them for a moment before he invites them to sit down. Reena goes to stand before the window, watching the scene. In a mumble.*] Oh, here you are. Sit down, all; sit down. [*Trying to be funny and show that he isn't ill-at-ease — after they have sat down.*] Well, shentlemens, what happy chance brings you all here?

Horawn. No chance; we come to fetch you.. You are now a Brother Repentant. [*To Kornavaun*] Give him his coat of th' Third Ordher.
    [*Kornavaun comes to Chatastray holding out the coat for him to don.*

Chatastray [*shoving the proffered coat aside*]. I wouldn't, I couldn't, wear that damned thing!

McGeelish [*after a silent pause*]. We didn't hear you, Chatastray; you didn't say anything.

Horawn. We have had a fireside chat with our Bishop, Chatastray, and he very softly and good-humouredly showed us the error of writing as we did.

McGeera. He gave us tea.

Bunny [*delightedly*]. An' shook us all be th' hand when we were leavin'.

Reena. Did he say anything about th' attack on little Noneen or th' battherin' given to Mr. Chatastray?

Horawn. That's over, an' bygones is bygones. Mr. Chatastray's keepin' Noneen here was wrong, an' he knows it now ; but doesn't bear any ill will — do you, Chatastray?

Chatastray. Oh, I suppose not.

McGeelish. Th' Bishop touched our hearts.

McGeera. Yes, an' opened our eyes.

Horawn. We know now that we have to be careful not to include a word in our writin' that might arouse any sinful desire.

Kornavaun. *Domine dirige nos.*

McGeera. Sex desire isn't easy to control, but it must be done, or be damned in Hell to all eternity. So says St. Paul.

McGeelish. Reading immoral literature makes conthrol almost impossible ; and our thought must ever be on a higher level.

Reena. Is sex then an evil thing?

Kornavaun. No, it isn't, for God made it in us ; but since he is th' maker, he only has th' right to tell when and how to use it, through th' ordinance of Holy Church.

[*A loud ring of the doorbell is heard.*

Chatastray [*to Reena*]. Please see who that is, dear.

[*She hurries out.*

Kornavaun [*cocking an ear*]. Dear ?
> [*After a pause, Reena comes back into the room followed by Noneen and Beoman.*

Reena. Here's Noneen and Mr. Beoman to say goodbye.

Chatastray. To say goodbye ?

Reena. They're off to England.

Chatastray [*sadness in his voice*]. Off to England ?

Kornavaun. Th' proper place for them.

Beoman [*to Chatastray*]. Wish you were comin' with us.

Chatastray [*to Beoman*]. Sit down, Martin, till I get through here, will you ?
> [*Beoman and Noneen sit down towards the back somewhere near Reena.*
> [*The writers all clasp their hands before their breasts in an attitude of silent prayer, and keep them so till the end of their talk.*

Beoman. Same company as before, but all in gala dress this evening.

Kornavaun [*angrily — to Beoman*]. Can't you say your damned goodbyes an' go !

Chatastray. This is my place, Kornavaun, not yours. Mr. Beoman is my guest, and stays here at my pleasure ; so sit down, and be quiet, [*after a pause*] or go.

Kornavaun [*growling*]. We don't want atheists here, disturbin' th' quiet land of Eireann.

McGeelish. No more disputin'. It's near th' time to be at th' startin'-point of th' Demonsthration, so we'd betther be goin'.

McGeera [*picking up the sackcloth coat meant for Chatastray, going over and offering it to him*]. Here you are, Chatastray ; put it on, [*with an attempt at easy humour*] an' show us how you look in it.

Chatastray [*taking it slowly and holding it hanging in his hand*]. No one could look anyway well in a thing like this.

Beoman [*quickly*]. No, nor feel well in it either. Are you goin' to insult your manhood be wearin' it afther what has been done to you ? To you and to Noneen ?

McGeelish. Th' use of a stick sometimes is good in turnin' a headsthrong man or woman from the wrong way into th' right one.

Kornavaun. That's well known — *argumentum baculinoleum.*

McGeera. Maybe we all needed a touch of it really.

Bunny. Th' Bishop's wise words were betther 'n any knock from a stick. Especially to you writers when he said that no writer can become great unless he always does it prosthrate on his belly before God.

Kornavaun. Ecce tempus idoneum.

McGeera [*to Chatastray*]. Go on, put th' damned thing on, an' let's be goin'.

Chatastray [*lifting it to put it on, when Reena seizes the coat and stops him*]. I suppose I must.

Reena [*as she seizes the coat*]. Don't, Dennis dear, don't do it.

Kornavaun [*suspiciously*]. ' Dennis, dear ' ? What's happenin' here ?

Reena. Remember what they've done to you ; you've lost your engineer and your best forewoman ; you've lost your American orders ; your factory is on three-quarter-time, and those who work there have had to be reduced by half ; don't put it on.

Chatastray [reassuringly]. Don't be alarmed, Reena, dear ; it's an odd coat, an' there can be no harm in thryin' it on.

Kornavaun. ' Reena, dear ' ?   Here, put th' coat on, man.
  [*Kornavaun gets hold of the coat, and pulls one arm of it on to Chatastray's ; as he is about to try to put Chatastray's other arm into it, Reena plucks it off the arm it's on.*

Reena. No, Dennis, no !

Kornavaun [thrusting the arm he's near into the coat]. Yes, Dennis, yes !

Reena [pulling it off again, jerking it from Kornavaun's hand, and flinging it with scorn to the floor]. No, darling ; this ugly flower is not for you to wear.

Beoman. It isn't a coat, Chatastray — it's a strait jacket. For God's sake, comrade, cast it from you !

Kornavaun [frantic]. Didja hear that !   Linkin' th' Communist name o' comrade with th' sacred name o' God ! An' no one stirs !

Horawn. Don't be a damned fool, Kornavaun.

Kornavaun. I'm not a fool !   You heard what he said, didn't youse ?   We're all Christians, aren't we ? Let's dhrive th' heretic outa th' house !

Bunny. Eh, there, easy, easy, man.

Kornavaun [*beside himself*]. An' that little whorish tanta-
liser into throuble, Noneen Melbayle with him, an'
get her leerin' gaudy gob far away from a vision of
innocent Christian eyes !

Beoman [*quietly — to the group*]. Silence th' hiss in this
viper-fool, or I shall !

Kornavaun [*frantic still — seizing Reena fiercely by the arm*].
And you, come away and get behind us, if you don't
want to fall into the wayward plight of Noneen
Melbayle !
> [*He tries to pull her away from Beoman and Chatastray,*
> *but she resists fiercely, breaks his hold on her, and hits*
> *him in the face, making him stagger back into the group.*

Reena [*angrily*]. You bordher-line lunatic, you full-
feathered hypocrite, you mouldy crumb of life, lay
no further hand on Reena or it will be th' worse for
you !

Chatastray [*sliding his arm around her waist*]. Now, now,
Reena, darling, be calm. There, now ; we'll leave th'
damned coat where 'tis, on th' floor of a quiet house in
th' quiet land of Eireann.

Kornavaun [*furious — pointing to Reena*]. Look at her, look
at her — a girl of th' Legion of Mary, an' look at her !
Skirt to th' knees, nylon stockin's, an' painted lips !
A jeering Jezebel ! When any modest boy ventures to
kiss a modest Legion of Mary girl, it isn't paint he'll
taste.

Chatastray [*loudly*]. Well, go an' kiss th' dhried-up
modest lips, an' be damned to you !

Horawn. Please, please ! Come, Chatastray, let us go to join th' Demonsthration, an' forget all about this sorry scene.

Chatastray. No.

Bunny [*enthusiastically*]. Yes ; let's all go — Beoman, Noneen, an' all !

Noneen
Chatastray
Beoman
Reena
    [*in chorus*]. No !

Kornavaun. Be God, you'll suffer for all this, Chatastray ! You'll lose your Irish ordhers as well as your American ones, an' your factory'll fall on your disobedient head.

McGeera. Oh, shut up, Kornavaun ! We don't want anything to happen like that, for Chatastray has always been a good friend to us writers.

Chatastray [*calmly*]. I've already lost most ordhers ; th' factory'll soon be no longer mine : I'm sellin' it.

Horawn [*aghast*]. You are ?

Chatastray. To a Northern Ireland mill-owner. He's taken over my American orders ; he's waitin' me final answer to his offer. Soon th' machinery'll be taken away, an' only th' walls left standin'.

Beoman [*sarcastically*]. It'll make a damned fine hall for th' Legion of Mary, or a place for you writers an' thinkers to lie on your bellies before God, an' write !

Kornavaun. Ha, jibe away, within th' little time left to you ! But you have to go, [*pointing to Chatastray*] an' it won't be long till he folleys you. [*Pointing to Reena*] Maybe, too, that one'll have to' flit too, unless she mends her ways, an' gets back to where she used to be, through th' dark tunnel of penance, prayer, an' fastin'. That's what we do to any atheist or Communist. We get them, don't we, boys? We run them in!

McGeelish. We run them in!

McGeera. We dhrive them forth!

Horawn [*more slowly*]. We cast them out!

Bunny [*impatiently*]. Come on, if youse are comin'. [*He looks at his wrist-watch.*] Th' time is near for us to be there.

> [*The whole group gather closer and turn towards the door to go.*

Horawn [*in a last appeal to Chatastray*]. Dennis, come with us. Don't be too foolish. You have still to live here. [*He takes up the yellow and white sash.*] Come and walk with your old friends whom you helped so often. [*He offers him the sash.*] Here, man, put this on you, an' never mind the damned sackcloth coat!

> [*Chatastray takes it from him, handles it hesitantly, while all the others watch him.*

Horawn [*encouragingly*]. Go on, Dennis, put it on.

Chatastray [*throwing it gently on to the table*]. No!

Kornavaun [*loudly and commandingly*]. Come on, boys, an' leave them now to what's comin' to them!

> [*They form up and march in a semi-processional manner from the room — two by two, or in file, one by one, if the door doesn't take two at a time — all but Horawn,*

B.G.C.—F

*who hesitates at the door, turns back to speak to Chata-
stray.*

Horawn [*appealingly*]. Sorry for all this, Dennis. [*A
pause.*] I'm gettin' out a small book o' poethry soon.
I wondher could you let me have a little to help — oh,
fifty quid would do. I don't like askin', you've been
so kind so often. No hurry, y'know — tomorrow'll
do fine ?

Chatastray [*quietly*]. I've given McGeelish help with a
novel he never wrote ; help to McGeera to get his
plays into a book ; an' help to you before to publish
bad verse. No more, Horawn, no more. [*A pause —
loudly*] Get out !

Horawn [*going to the door and turning to face Chatastray on the
threshold — venomously*]. Kornavaun was right — you are
a bit of a bastard after all !

[*He goes out, slamming the door after him.*

Beoman. Th' tumult an' th' shouting dies, so there's
nothing left to do now but say goodbye.

Chatastray. Sure you're doin' wisely, Noneen ?

Beoman. Noneen'll be all right. She'll stop with me
married sister an' me till she settles into a job, an'
afther, if she wants to.

Noneen [*shyly — to Chatastray*]. Goodbye, sir, I'll always
remember you for your goodness to me, so kind you
were, standin' between me an' me father when he was
beside himself with dhrink.

Chatastray [*with feeling*]. Goodbye, dear Noneen. I loved
you as I'd love a daughter if I had one, an' I don't like
to see you go.

Noneen. I have to go.   Anyway, I won't be noticed in th' crowd.   [*More shyly still, she offers him the gramophone record she has been carrying.*]   I'd liketa give you this.   I thought you might play it now an' again, an' remember me.   You remember how you got me to like folk-music an' song, an' this was my favourite for a long time.   Remember it?

Chatastray [*trying hard to remember*]. There were so many of them, Noneen.

Noneen. Th' one we used oftenest;   I sang it while you played on th' piano!

Chatastray. Yes;   let me see — was it ' I saw from the Beach '?

Noneen [*delighted*]. Yes, yes!   You *did* remember.   [*He takes the record from her.*]   So now, goodbye!

Chatastray. Let's play it once as a farewell before you go, dear.   [*He puts the record on the gramophone.*

Noneen. No, no, Mr. Chatastray;   I couldn't bear to hear it now.

Beoman. We'll go — goodbye.   Take good care of dear Reena.   [*He shakes Chatastray's hand.*   [*To Reena*] Good-bye, Reena.   [*He shakes hers.*

Noneen [*throwing herself into the arms of Reena*]. Goodbye, goodbye!

[*They embrace and kiss each other.*

Reena. Write to me, Noneen, and tell me all that happens to you.   Maybe I'll go over to see you some day.

Noneen. Oh, do, oh, do, Reena !

[*They go to the door. Chatastray goes to Noneen.*

Chatastray. Write to me, too, Noneen. Goodbye, once more, an' may God be ever near you. [*He bends down and kisses her cheek.*] You were once my daughter. [*Beoman and Noneen go.*] All alone again, Reena.

[*He takes up the yellow and white sash from the table and fiddles with it ; Reena watches him doing it.*

Reena. Leave that alone, an' come here an' kiss me.

Chatastray. Oh, Reena !

[*He comes forward shyly, puts his arm around her, and gives her a sincere but quiet kiss.*

Reena. Don't go on meddling with that sash — it is a concern of ours no longer.

Chatastray. Of course not ; all th' same, Reena, I'm thirty-five years old, an' this sash is a symbol of all I believe an' all th' customs I'm used to throughout them years.

Reena. Well, I'm twenty-six, but nine years behind, an' unity of companionship can turn them back to nine weeks only. What will you do now ?

Chatastray. Oh, if I sell th' factory I'll have enough to keep me going for some years. The mill-owner who bought my factory offered me a job in his, but I refused.

Reena. Oh, Dennis, that was a mistake. You can't stay here.

Chatastray [*doubtfully*]. I suppose not, but this place is all I ever knew, an' it will be hard to break away from it.

Reena. Tens of thousands, boys an' girls, have done it ; no harder for you than it was for them.   If you stay here, you must have someone with you.   After hospital duties, I can cook a simple meal for both of us ; and, on my free day, we can have a good time together.

Chatastray. Good God, no, Reena — not afther what happened to me an' Noneen !

Reena. It won't happen to me, an' if they should try any thuggish thricks, there'll be an afterglow that'll singe th' whole damned town !

Chatastray [*fiddling again with the yellow and white sash*]. I — I couldn't allow that, Reena ; I really couldn't.

Reena. You could and you must.   Either that, or th' North or England.   And do stop fondling that damned sash ; that doesn't mean a thing to us now ! [*Outside in the street, tramping feet are heard, and a band playing ' Faith of our Fathers '.   They listen for a moment, then Reena goes to the window, and looks out at what is happening.   Chatastray takes up the sash again.   Looking out at the crowd, she lilts a verse of what the band is playing*] :
>Faith of our fathers, we will love
>Both friend an' foe in all our sthrife ;
>An' preach thee too as love knows how,
>By kindly words and virtuous life.

Well, Reena an' Dennis have had a fine example of their virtuous life an' kindly words !   There they go, th' lot o' them, marching !   Go on, go on ; you go [*gesturing to the right*] that way to th' right ; we go this way [*gesturing with her hand*] to th' left.   [*Chatastray has slid the sash around his shoulder, and slides slowly towards the door, picking up the yellow and white rosette from the table.   He opens the door softly, and goes out, leaving the door open behind him. She stretches an arm backward with a hand extended.*] Here, come here, Dennis, an' let's both stand hand in hand silently defying them as they all go marching by ! [*After a pause.*] Come on, Dennis ; look at them, and have the laugh of your life ! [*She stays looking out for a moment, then sensing something wrong, wheels around, and sees that Dennis has gone. She notices that the sash and rosette are gone too. She runs to the door and calls out. At the door*] Dennis, Dennis ! [*There is no answer. She hurries to the window, and looks out on to the street below.*] Oh, there he goes, sash an' all on him, rushing along to overtake his frightened friends. [*She leaves the window, and comes into the room.*] My Dennis is gone from me ; poor frightened fool ! [*She notices the sackcloth coat — mockingly*] Oh, God, he's left his fancy coat behind him ! [*The door opens suddenly, and Beoman comes in quickly. He sees that Reena is agitated, and stands there near the door, half-gaping at her. When she sees him — angrily.*] What the hell brings you here now ?

Beoman [*apologetically*]. Sorry, Miss Reena. Me and Noneen stopped below to watch a band go by, and we saw your Mr. Chatastray rushing after th' procession, with the sash round him — what's happened ?

Reena [*a little brokenly*]. He's gone ! Poor frightened Dennis ! He saved his soul at the eleventh hour. [*Bitterly*] My God, what would have happened to me harnessed to him for life ! Well, he saved my soul too. [*She breaks down, sinks on a chair, and buries her face in her hands.*] Oh, Dennis, Dennis ! Oh, Martin !

Beoman [*coming to her, gently and timidly placing a hand on her head*]. Later on, you'll be glad this happened.

Reena [*angrily and resentfully*]. Oh, how th' hell do you know whether I will or no ! [*Taking his hand from her head.*] And don't you give me your thin pity, please.
[*He goes over to the gramophone, and fiddles timidly with the record.*

Beoman. No, of course not. Why should you ? You're not the one to give in. I should have known.

Reena [*exasperated*]. Oh, shut up ! [*A pause.*] Where's Noneen ?

Beoman. Noneen ?   Oh, Noneen — below, beside the door ; waiting. She's awright. [*A pause.*] What are you going to do — stay here ?

Reena [*waking up — surprised*]. Here ? Stay here ? He'll never have me behind his green curtains again — th' mouse !

Beoman [*bright again*]. Wee, sleekit, cow'rin, tim'rous beastie, O, what a panic's in thy breastie ! Went after his boys of the cold brigade like th' hammers of hell.

Reena [*sharply*]. There, that's enough about him. You go back to Noneen. No reason to bother about me.

Beoman. No, of course not. I'm going now. [*A pause, but he makes no move.*] This is the record that was Noneen's first favourite. What's this it was ? [*He looks at title.*] ' I saw from the Beach ' — ah, Moore's ; yes. Well, I'm going now. [*She doesn't answer.*] Are you staying here — I mean in Ballybeedhust ?

Reena [*tonelessly*]. I don't know ; don't know what to do.

Beoman [*awkwardly*]. No ? [*A pause*]. Why not come with me ?

Reena [*staring at him — startled*]. Go with you ?

Beoman. With us, I mean ; Noneen and me. Noneen would be delighted.

Reena. Noneen likes me, I know. [*Rougishly*] Do you like me, too ?

Beoman [*very simply*]. I think I love you, Reena.

Reena [*rising from her chair and going to him — moved*]. Martin !
    [*She takes his head in her hands, then kisses him. He rather pulls his face away from hers, startled and much embarrassed, and becomes more intent with the gramophone. She watches him amusedly.*

Beoman [*awkwardly*]. Yes, it's a fine machine. Pity he didn't give it to Noneen.

Reena. There's me for you — I thought you'd like it.

Beoman. Like it ? Like what ?

Reena. The kiss, of course.

Beoman [*more embarrassed still*]. Oh, that ? Oh, that was over quick.

Reena. Did you expect it to last longer ?

Beoman. Me ? Oh, no ; not really. Not at all. [*He concentrates on the gramophone.*] One of Noneen's favourites, this one was. Yes. [*He starts it playing, and the song rings out*] :
I saw from the beach, when the morning was shining,
A bark o'er the waters move gloriously on.
I came when the sun from that beach was declining,
The bark was still there, but the waters were gone.

Reena [*stopping the record with a swift movement*]. Oh, God damn the song ! It isn't true anyway. The peace of a dusk is often as good, and sometimes better, than the shine of the morning.

Beoman. Of course not. A pleasant air, all the same, Miss Reena.

Reena [*very serious*]. Mr. Beoman, listen ! Catholics, Protestants, and you unbelievers, seem to be frightened fools !

Beoman. Oh ?

Reena [*more gently*]. So now you'd better give back what I gave you.

Beoman [*wondering*]. What you gave me, Miss Reena ?

Reena. Yes — the kiss.

Beoman [*bewildered for a moment, then seeing her smiling face, he roughly and warmly clasps her in his arms, and kisses her*]. There it is, Reena, darling ; and another one for good measure.

Reena [*breaking away, gently*]. You've forgotten Noneen.

Beoman. Oh, God, so I have ! I'll go to her.

Reena. Are you leaving me here ?

Beoman. No ; you're coming with me !

Reena. With *me* !

Beoman. I'll carry you off, and Noneen is coming with us.

Reena [*as he makes to carry her*]. You mustn't tussle me, Martin. [*She frees herself from his arms.*] We've a few things to do before we go — to leave the room as he'd like to find it when he returns to the safety behind th' green curtains. [*She goes to the window.*] You put on th' light, [*he does so*] and come to th' other curtain. We'll close th' world out together, and meet in th' centre. [*He goes to the curtain opposite from her end.*] Now ! [*Each pulls a curtain till both meet. Releasing his end Beoman embraces Reena.*]

Reena [*gently releasing herself*]. Th' shy, bashful man has become quite a stormy one, hasn't he ?

Beoman [*impatiently*]. Oh, darling, let's go from this dead place.

Reena [*going to the gramophone*]. Let th' song sing its heart out first, Martin.   [*She starts it off.*
        And such is the fate of our life's early promise,
        So passing the springtide of joy we have known :

Beoman [*switching off the light*]. Let it sing in th' darkness alone ! I'll wait no longer ! [*He snatches her in his arms, and carries her towards the door.*]

Reena [*putting an arm around his neck and kissing him*]. Martin, dear, what a stormy Romeo you are !
        [*The gramophone goes on playing as he carries her out by the door.*
    Each wave that we danced on at morning, ebbs from us
    And leaves us, at eve, on the bleak shore alone.

END OF THE PLAY

FIGURO IN THE NIGHT

In Two Scenes eloquently and humorously related,
but vilely and maliciously inspired and created
by dangerous and unseemly influences emanating
from, and begotten in, the pernicious confines
of atheistic and communistic lands

DEADICATION

To a Postage Stamp, one printed by an Astonished Hungary of a Young Lad, in the Form of a Statue, doing an Obscene and Most Indecent Action under the Guise of an Innocent Fountain, seen, apparently for the First Time by the Embarrassed Hungarians, near the Grand' Place of Brussels, Capital City of Catholic Belgium, when they attended the International Exhibition there in 1958.

———

This Work is prayerfully and solemnly dedicated to what is known as ' The Ferocious Chastity of Ireland ', and has been written and printed for the one and only reason of warning to Gael, Gall-Gael, and Gael-Gall, including those decent and law-abiding members of that section of the Irish Community who live, work, and worship within a religion and political belief contrary to, and at enmity with, the life, worship, and political activities of those domiciled within what is regarded as the twenty-six counties of Southern Ireland ; in the abiding hope that all, North and South, will combine against, fight, and destroy this communist and insidious effort to overthrow the age-long virtue of the Irish People ; to prevent this rock-built chastity from corrosion, so that it may outlive all red-like attempts to frighten or weaken its determination by a godless and ruthless ridicule. Amen.

'There is no greater curse on the good spirit of any parish than a collection of old maids and bachelors living in homes, and living the disappointed lives that these people live, doing no good for themselves and for the Church and for the future of the parish.'—A Roman Catholic Bishop of Derry, reported in *The Irish Press*, Labour Day, 1959.

'In a school district of Irish-speaking Conamara, is one where fifty houses stand without one woman or one child, but bachelors only. Responsible for this unnatural story here and many another district, too, is the unreasonable Puritanism that is put in force upon the young.

'The place of least enjoyment is the place of least engagements towards marriage. If gaiety and enjoyment are hidden from the young, the young will go to where they are to be found.'—Chriostóir Mhic Aonghusa, broadcasting over Radio Eireann, according to an article in Gaeilge, 'Conamara Inné agus Inniu'—'Conamara Today and Yesterday', appearing in *The Irish Press*.

O'Casey Question : Is it going to be *Conamara Yesterday Today and Forever* ?

SCENE I

*As the scene opens the tune of the chorus of ' Love's Old Sweet Song'
is sounding, faintly at first, then clearly, fading away again when
the characters begin to speak ; and, maybe, a voice or two singing
it in the background.*

*A street of one- or two-storey houses in a district just on the
environs of Dublin ; a new district, part of the city borough.
An Obelisk to the memory of men who fell in the Great War
stands at one end of street ; a Keltic Cross to the memory of men
who fought and fell for Ireland stands at the other end. The
houses are dark, the blinds down, and no light showing, save in
one window in the lower part of the centre house. The blind is
down, too, over this window, but it is of thin material, and
shows the shadow of a young girl standing or sitting close by
Once, she pulls the blind aside, and tries to peer out into the
darkness ; then lets the blind fall back again into its place. The
street is lonely-looking, and no sound is heard. It is late
evening, and a pale moon over the house gives a ghostly glow
to the street. A few moments pass, then the door of the centre
house opens, and the Young Girl stands within its frame,
clearly seen by the light shining from the hall. She is pretty,
but her face is pale and more worn than her young years should
show. She is dressed in a bright-red skirt, a black jumper
showing a white throat and part of a white bosom ; she wears
black stockings and black shoes. She has a worried look, and
looks up and down the silent street.*

Young Girl. Ne'er a one in sight. No one goin' up the
   street, no one comin' down it. Silent night, unholy

night ; yet me heart is warm with a curious feelin' of
delightful hope. [*She sings*]:
  The houses are empty, the night it is fallin',
  Not a child in a house either silent or bawlin' ;
  There isn't a single bird even left callin',
  Since all have gone off to the fair.
[*She looks about her again.*] Not a louse stirrin'. [*She
looks toward the Keltic Cross standing to the right.*] Keltic
Cross to the memory of three heroes who died for
Ireland. [*She looks towards the six-foot Obelisk to the left.*]
A pillar or slab to the memory of the twenty men who
died for England on Flanders field. All near kids, an'
not one of them ever got a chance to whip a girl off her
feet and lay her down flat in a silent nook to — Saints
above, what am I thinkin', what am I sayin' ! [*She
sings again*] :
  My Johnny, he wanted to stay here an' mind me.
  But in what state o' dhress would me ma 'n' da
    find me ?
  They'd hustle me inta me room, an' then bind me,
  When they hurried home from the fair.

  Dear me, what can the matter be ?
  Dear, dear, what can the matter be ?
  I wish Johnny was back from the fair !

  I've promised my heart a time of good kissin',
  Kissin', good kissin' ;
  With nothin' that's lively an' lovely left missin',
  When Johnny comes back from the fair !
[*She begins to close the door.*]
  Dear, dear, what can the matter be ?
[*As she goes in and the door closes.*]
  Johnny's so long at the fair.

[*A very Old Woman enters slowly, walking with shaky
steps. She is badly bent, and pokes her way along with
a stick. She is enveloped in a drab brown dress,
gathered in at the middle with a black cord. A black
cowlish scarf covers her head and almost hides her face,
which is, when seen, pale, thin, bony ; her eyes sunken,
her lips cracked, her cheeks hollow ; like a face that has
been fondled by the hand of death. As she comes in she is
singing in a low and very old voice, though the words are
heard distinctly.*]

Old Woman [*singing*] :
    He promis'd to buy me a bunch of blue ribbons,
    Blue ribbons, blue ribbons ;
    He promis'd to buy me a bunch of blue ribbons,
    To tie up my bonnie brown hair.
He did, too ; long, long ago. I have them still, but
the blue in them's gone yella ; yes, yella. I never
wore them. Ma and Da said I was too young for
titivation. Always too young. Jimmy's song, too :
we're too young to marry yet. Always expectin' till
all expectin' died. [*She goes over slowly to the Cross of the
Heroes, and sits down on the steps to the pedestal. Chanting
in her old quavering voice*] ;
    Oh dear, what can the matter be ?
    Dear, dear, what can the matter be ?
What the hell does it matter what the matter is . . .
now ! Over an' done with.
    [*An Old Man half totters, half creeps, in from the opposite
    side to where the woman is sitting. He helps himself
    along with a stick in either hand. He is dressed in dirty
    drab brown clothing, coat and trousers too big for him,
    and they hang around his thin legs and half cover his
    shaking hands. He wears a cap of the same dull colour.*
B.G.C.——G

He comes in muttering to himself, his back bent and his head bent lower than his back.

Old Man. Yis. I'm riskin' things coming out a night like this, but there's some strange stir about. I saw it in the sky looking east. Like fireworks or something. Centre o' the city somewhere. What can the matter be? Not that I care a damn really what th' matter is. Give a sneeze in Dublin, and a crowd gathers. [*He slowly raises his head, and looks around.*] Here, just here, before these monuments was stuck up, I first met — what was her name now? Nora, I think; No, not Nora. Can't remember. Oh, years and years ago. Haven't seen sight of her for a long time; years and years. She near got me. Buying blue ribbons for to tie up her bonnie brown hair. Imagine it! What a gobeen I was them days! Wanted to make out it meant marryin'. Tryin' to tie me to her forever be a bunch of blue ribbons. God be praised I had a sensible ould father. Sent her leppin' about her own business. A sound man. Worked his twenty acres, two roods, and a perch till he was ninety; kept it up till he was found dead in a furrow and the two horses draggin' the plough round anyhow. Didn't marry till he was 56. A sound man.

Old Woman [*mumbling*]. Wonder who's mutterin' over there? [*More clearly*] Here I met him first, now that I think of it; yes, right here. Can't for th' life o' me think what his name was now. Too far away. Shy, both of us, not sure to go on or go back. That was the way all the time — going on, stepping back, till we went back too far, and the years flowed between what had been, and the blue ribbons faded. God's will, and all for the best. A pitiful sowing that gave no crop ; only a tiny leaf that died in a day.

Old Man. Wonder who's mutterin' t'other side ? The land never got loose from the family. I have it still ; fast within these two fit hands. Some spuds, onions, cabbage, and a pig, leavin' the rest of it to God. Ay, and a fair young man still.

Old Woman [*making several attempts to rise before she gets to her feet*]. Uh, uh ! Must make another spurt forward.
                              [*She walks slowly towards Old Man.*

Old Man [*making several efforts before rising stiffly*]. Might as well put another mile behind me.   [*The two meet.*

Old Woman [*to the Old Man*]. 'Scuse me, sir, but d'ye happen to know what's afoot in Dublin this night ?

Old Man. Don't know, good woman, but I'm on me way to find out.

Old Woman. If y'are, you're going the wrong way, good man.

Old Man [*a little testily*]. I am, am I ? Maybe you know the right one ?

Old Woman. The way I'm going, for I'm bent on finding out what it is.

Old Man. The light an' the sounds come from where I'm goin', woman.

Old Woman. From where I'm goin', for I seen and heard them.

Old Man. I know where I'm goin', see ? Maybe, ma'am, you'd try to mind your own business.
                              [*He makes to go his way.*

Old Woman. I might ha' known that a born lady shouldn't sully herself be scatterin' a greeting to a low-born tramp !

Old Man [*wheeling back — angrily*]. Tramp is it ! Easy seen you don't know who you're facin' ! Tramp ! I'll have you know this tramp's one o' the degenetors of a one that sat on his own broad bench of lordship, chief of the Barony of Cassignavar.

Old Woman. Like me, yes ; just like meself : a lady highborn, with pressure of gardens, orchards, and much cattle around me ; singers and dancers came and went ; bright things glistened everywhere in the manor I lived in, and life was like an apple ripening under a happy sun, an' no young head shawled.

Old Man. Same as me, Cis. Good-looking ones, peace on their lips, fresh in the dew of younger years, came knocking at me door, even tapping at me window, but I kept to me prayers, and used the ribbons bought for some of them as markers in the holy books I read to provoke a sound contrition. I was a great and mighty wondher to all them who lived around me.

Old Woman. I dunno about using ribbons, meant for brown curls or raven thresses, for marking places in the holy books ; I dunno that the holy lads who wrote the holy books could feel up to the marks with gay ribbons, fit only for a girl's ringlets, or for decorating dainty pieces shelthering the pleasant and secret parts of a lassie's virgin form, entangling themselves through the holy words written down in a holy book.

Old Man. Wouldn't it show up a victory of spirit over flesh, woman ? The holy writers would be pleased and the saints would be proud.

Old Woman. Did the same meself ; chose the betther parts. This little hand o' mine flutthered a farewell to many a minsthrel boy, many a brennan o' the moor, many a horseman of dunrone ; this little hand, a tiny bit wrinkled now, flutthered a goodbye to them all.

Old Man. And me ; many a maid of a sweet brown knowe, many a rose of Tralee, many a lovely Kate of Liskehaun, many a cailin deas crúite na mbó ; but I turned away from petticoat an' bodice, an' banished meself brightly under a bishop's blessing. Always fateful to meself ; in God's hands ; it never thundhered where I was.

Old Woman. Nor where I was, either. Dead quiet wherever I went. Thry as I did in a moment of forgetting, I never heard a bird sing. Once only, sitting be a window, when I fingered me fading blue ribbons, I thought I heard a blackbird's whistle : imagination. No, thank God, in the house or out of it, I never heard a birdsong to disthract me from me higher thinking.

Old Man. Now I think of it, nor me either. Listening to what God and His holy Church is saying, even a bird singing can be an occasion for sin.

Old Woman. For the bird, good man ?

Old Man. For everyone ; for me, too, and you as well. Look to yourself when you begin to enjoy a thing. I'm going. [*He moves as if going ; stops, and turns to her again.*] What was it you said ? Blue ribbon. Why should you think a blue ribbon would start a blackbird's whistlin' ?

Old Woman. Me own blue ribbons. Them I got to wear and never wore.

Old Man. Why blue ? What's in blue any more'n any other colour ?

Old Woman. To me, yes ; to me, memory, the blackbird's song, and a boy.

Old Man. Oh, a boy, eh ?

Old Woman. Yis ; me mother saved me from wearing them.

Old Man. Me father stopped me once from fixing blue ribbons in a girl's hair.

Old Woman. Me mother ; your father.

Old Man. Your mother ; me father.

Old Woman⎫
⎬ [*together*]. ⎰ May they rest in peace, the both of them. They saved us both from throuble and satisfied reflections.
Old Man ⎭

   [*The cawing of a crow comes down clear from the sky, and both look up together.*

Old Woman. A crow ! Out late. What brings him out alone like that ?

Old Man. I don't like it. Three caws it gave ; caw [*pause*] caw, [*pause*] caw — just like that.

Old Woman. Was it a crow, d'ye think ?

Old Man. Didn't you hear the caws, woman ?

Old Woman. I didn't see the bird.

Old Man. Nor did I ; but I heard the caw. There's it again — listen !

   [*Again the caws are heard — three of them ; each some time after the one before ; Caw . . . caw . . . caw !*

Old Woman. Well ?   The caw's no different from any other caw.

Old Man. But where did the caw come from ?

Old Woman. Come from ?   From the crow, of course.

Old Man. What crow ?   I seen no crow.

Old Woman. He musta been there or he couldn't have cawed.

Old Man. Aah !   He shoulda been there, you mean ; but he wasn't.

Old Woman. Where was he then ?   If the bird wasn't with the caw, where did the caw come from ?

Old Man. An agency ;   some dark agency ;   somewhere.

Old Woman. Where ?   Not in either of us, anyway.

Old Man. Y'never know.   Whisht !
  [*Again the caws are heard — one . . . two . . . three.*

Old Woman. There they go again !

Old Man. Three caws ;   three times three caws — a black-magic Angelus !   And no bird visible.   How did they come ?   God help us, we're all in it !

Old Woman. What's up with you ?   All in what ? How're we all in what ?

Old Man. All in the caws.   The caws come.   There's no bird anywhere.   We heard the caws, and we're the only figures about resembling birds.

Old Woman. Excuse me, good man, but I'm not letting meself be anyway like a crow.

Old Man. You heard the caws plain, didn't you ? So did I, so they musta come from within ourselves ; we musta cawed without knowing it.

Old Woman. Cawed without knowing it ? We're not birds ; not even distantly related to a crow. How could a caw come from either of us ?

Old Man. Be engenceration, woman. We musta been tranced into having our ears closed to all natural sounds, an' opened to hear what wasn't in the outside world, but a feeling ensconced within us somewhere, and giving uttherance to a warning of nine cawses within our feelings that our ears heard, shifting us to a way of watching for some dangerous loosening of some sacred habit or tradition or practice livening up in us, in most, maybe in all of us. So the caws came out of us, warning, warning, without us feeling them come, but our ears open to the sounds seemingly outside of us, up above, but really through our own ears seeking out our souls.

Old Woman. Your thoughts is too weighty for common minds, man. What funny fury or uncommon peace could happen here ?

> [*The upper window of the house in which is the Young Girl opens ; she glances out, then goes from the window ; but her voice is heard singing clearly.*

Young Girl.
Oh, when he comes back with the bonnie blue ribbons,
Oh, then will my love be all bright and a-daring,
A clasping, a kissing, an' a bosom a-baring,
When he ties up my bonnie brown hair !

Old Man. There 'tis ! The girl in the house waiting ; the boy at the fair to buy her ribbons of blue.

Old Woman [*dreamily chanting*]. To tie up her bonnie brown hair.

Old Man. There 'tis ! We all know what happens when he ties up her bonnie brown hair ! That's what'll shatther the counthry and toss her soul to perdition. Our life-long misery began when Adam tied a blue ribbon on the bonnie brown hair of his Eve.

Old Woman. The poor man got tired looking at her dressed only in her innocence ; he needed her to look gayer to him and feel gayer herself, for the heady juice of the apple they'd eaten jollied them into a jostle together.

Old Man. That's it ! Our desthruction ! Oh, woman, what're you commending ?

Old Woman. Adam an' Eve had to sthrike out for themselves, hadn't they ? They couldn't easily forever sit undher a breadfruit, undher a banyan, undher a bamboo tree, in a garden, eating grapes, could they ?

Old Man. God forgive you, woman ! No wondher dark things are happening, with God knows what kinda spirits walking the streets along with the ghost of Molly Malone. A garden is a lovesome thing, God wot, and that was God's own garden, woman.

Old Woman. God's wot what ?

Old Man. What God's what's what ?

Old Woman. I'm asking you what's God's whot ?

Old Man. How can I tell what's God's whot's wot ? It's what's not your what's whot or my wot's what. Only God wots what His own wot is.

Old Woman. You're thinking so high that you don't know even what's your own whot's wot, or mine, or even Adam and Eve's, who well knew what was whot when she wove thread from a lamb's fleece into strips that Adam coloured a rich blue from the juice of an herb growing among the radishes, using the strips to brighten the lustre of her bonnie brown hair.

Old Man. Oh, woe, woe, woad woe.

Old Woman. Adam knew his what's whot, for he woad and he woo'd her.

Old Man. And lost his stattus and ruined us all and lost his loneliness, left lonely in the lovely garden they had to leave behind them. He woad and woo'd and won great woe for all !

Old Woman. Well, welcome woe, for it took man off his guard and sent him out to seek things and get things done. The fruit from the tree of knowledge of good and evil set us free from coddling, and gave us the pain and the power to do our own thinking, walk on our own feet ; clap our own hands at what ourselves had done. The lush laziness of the garden lovely was sappin' our life away.

Old Man. Hush and hold your peace, woman, [*he makes the sign of the Cross*] for that like o' talk will make the world here wobble, and set the stars into a thremble, though they are too far off to hear a word.

Old Woman [*dreamily*]. Adam an' Eve had to rise up and get away from the thymy scents and the spicy flavours flowing from the trees sweating sweet gums that took movement from the limbs and sent the mind into a drowsy silence.

Old Man. Hush, woman, I tell you ! God's favour was in the spicy breezes, and His voice spoke from the drowsy silence.

Old Woman. They needed a fresher air to breathe. Tired of an everlasting life within an everlasting lullaby. Away from the floating scents of musk to the hardier smell of sea, of heather, and of a pinewood. To hear other voices than God's and their own.

Old Man. Kyrie eleison, Christe eleison ! Woman, be silent, for God's sake !

Old Woman. Man chose the distress of sweat on his face rather than oil of balsam anointing a white skin. That was the way it went, and angels were left flying over an empty garden, for man was gone ; left the mighty beat of their wings for the gentle whirr of the linnet's wing over his head in the dusk of an evening.

Old Man. With death for the linnet and death for the man.

Old Woman. Death for this man, death for that woman, but greater life for all.

Old Man. Be it less or more, or soon or slow, to that same lot, however mean or high, Time leads safe on to the grave.

Old Woman. Life with a lover and his lass sits singing on the tomb, and mocks the stone.

Old Man. Oh, you fool ! It is this lover and his lass, the fire in the pair of them, that gives the flame to the sword carried by the angel keeping the gateway to the holy garden ; this lust for the golden apples of the sun on the part of the one, and the lust for the silver apples of the moon on the part of the other, that keeps us from finding a way back to the destiny of innocence once again.

Old Woman. The farther we get away from the garden, the better. It was outside of it that the mind grew and the hands got their cunning. I hope that the commotion stirring somewhere in Dublin to-night means another step away from where we once were.

> [*Again the window of the house is opened, and the half-figure of the Young Girl appears, looking out into the street, as she sings a verse softly :*
> With love in me heart an' dear Johnny beside me,
> I'd dare an' I'd do ; I'd do an' I'd dare ;
> He'd be welcome to ruffle the saucy blue ribbon
> That tied up my bonnie brown hair.
> [*She looks out for a moment, slowly closes the window again, and disappears from view.*
> [*Here the tune of the chorus of ' Love's Old Sweet Song ' is heard, not loudly, and it goes on till Scene ends.*

Old Man. You see ? Still wailing for the blue ribbons. And you, yes, you would sanction and sing over the departure of all that is holy, all that has flowed from safe tradition, of all that is of good report.

Old Woman. Of all that is spent, that has withered, of all that is of no earthly use today.

Old Man. The father is still king of the family, the mother the queen.

Old Woman. The oul' fella's no longer lord of the family. They are but cracked china figaries on the mantelshelf of memory.

Old Man. Back to the Garden, I say ; with hasty steps or slow, it's all in all to go back to the Garden !

Old Woman. Farther and farther away from it ! There can be no life left but for the letting down and the lifting up.

Old Man. Lifting up and letting down what ?

Old Woman. Letting trousers down and lifting skirts up !

Old Man. I won't listen, I won't !

Old Woman. Under the berried bushes or under the bamboo tree.

Old Man. We risk our souls' salvation talking. Let us go to where the stir in Dublin is.

Old Woman. I go the high road.

Old Man. And I go with you.

Old Woman. At this time o' night ? No, John, no. Seen together under the darkened stars, what would they say about us only that there was no good in our minds ?

Old Man. You're right !

Old Woman. I have to keep my reputation well in hand, so go your way while I go mine. [*They go out slowly and limpingly in different directions, the Old Woman pausing suddenly on her way.*] My God, what was I sayin' a minute ago ! Dhreamin' I was — a bad, bad dhream ! Thro' me fault, thro' me most grievous fault ! [*singing low as she goes*] ;

        Oh, dear, what can the matter be ?
        There's something quite odd in the air ;
        Oh, dear, what can the matter be,
        Th' world has gone off to the fair !

Scene II

The scene is the same as before. Somehow, the place is much brighter, the doors of the houses and the windows are all gaily painted in red, blue, yellow, white, green, and orange. The great moon filling half the seen sky floods the scene with a full, graceful, and delightful glow. The bare trees of the former scene are full of foliage, and many-coloured fruits, shining like lighted globes, hang from some of them. Birds sing cheerily, and in the distance we hear the faint, pleasant lowing of cattle, gentle baaing of sheep, and the challenging crow of the cock. All the windows of the houses are lighted up, glowing red, green, or with variegated gleams, according to the patterns of the curtains stretched across them. Everything seems wonderful to eyes that see and ears that hear. Away in a distant part of the city a hubbub is heard, mostly subdued like quiet parts of a symphony, but now and again it swells into a deep agitated but confident musical murmur, loud and deep, pierced with several angry tones threatening something, defiant ; then fades again into the quietly-agitated musical murmur.

From the Obelisk hangs a wreath of red poppies ; from the Cross hangs a wreath of laurel dotted with white lilies. A few steps around each form a simple pedestal.

1st Old Man totters in from the left as 2nd Old Man totters in from the right. They stumble past each other, the 1st Old Man going to the Cross, the other going to the Obelisk, sitting down stiffly and carefully, with a few groans, one on the steps of the Cross, the other on the steps of the Obelisk, facing each other. The one by the Cross has his head bandaged, the one on the Obelisk has an arm in a sling. Their clothes are badly

*torn, and hang in shreds from their bodies. The one by the
Cross has been dressed half town, half country ; rough tweed,
with a black cravat round his neck ; the one by the Obelisk
wears a collar, but one end has been torn from its button, and
sticks out from his neck ; he wears a bowler hat, but it has been
badly dented ; the other wears a cap. They bend their bodies
over their knees wearily, and stay silent for a few moments.*

1st Old Man. Well, Mr. Tynan, well ?

2nd Old Man. Well, yourself, Michael Murphy ; well,
yourself.

1st Old Man. It's the end, Mr. Tynan ; it's the end.
Worse'n th' Black an' Tans.

2nd Old Man. A bod end, Michael Murphy ; a bod end.
Warse thon Wipers or th' run from Mons.

1st Old Man [*touching the Cross*] ⎫ [*together*]. ⎧They didn't
2nd Old Man [*touching the Obelisk*]⎭   ⎩die for this !

1st Old Man. The moon's afraid to come out, and the
night's as dark as it would be with the lost in the Day
of Judgement.

2nd Old Man. The heart of the summer is in it, yet the
leaves all fall from the trees, and the branches shiver
and shrivel up.

1st Old Man. The birds is dumb, their bakes agape with a
husky gasping.

2nd Old Man. The solid earth beneath us bumping up and
down.

1st Old Man. The cliffs of the coast crumbling, the
slopes of the mountains slithering down.

2nd Old Man. The workers idle, out seeking the horrible emotion of a minute's joy.

1st Old Man. The girls lurid with longing, racing away from decency, out to see a sight temerarious.

2nd Old Man. To see what they blush to name and love to handle.

1st Old Man. Hush! Don't let the handle of its name defile our minds.

2nd Old Man. Bringing disaster. The sea stays where it is, never coming closer, never going farther away.

1st Old Man. The ships on it standing still, without a stir or motion.

2nd Old Man. Like painted ships upon a painted ocean.

1st Old Man. The cattle in every byre low angrily, sheep baa balefully, whenever a church clock strikes the hour.

2nd Old Man. We're gonners, Mr. Murphy.

1st Old Man ⎱ *[together].* ⎰ It's the end, the end of all things
2nd Old Man ⎰   ⎱ here.

1st Old Man. We shouldn't have gone.

2nd Old Man. How right y'are! I very near vanished. Caught in the crowd, I got decorated for death, so I did.

1st Old Man. Am I any better? With any life worth livin' plucked and pounded outa me! Am I any better? Answer me that, Mr. Tynan.
    [*A Young Man staggers in, his clothes torn, his face scratched and bleeding a little. He staggers over to a doorway, and leans against the side of a door.*

Young Man [*pantingly*]. Them bitches of girls tore at me till I near lost possession of meself. Till I battled them down, getting rid of their tearing grips, I thought I'd lose me decent dangling accessory, so I did ! God forgive me.

1st Old Man. Whisht, whisht ! Don't give in now, young man !

2nd Old Man. How did it get there ? Did it fly down or did it climb up ? Is it now that miracles of Light is being offset now be miracles of Darkness ? The Civic Guard taking up point duty at the crack o' dawn saw it first and fainted. Now lying stark in hospital, with nothing left but a feeble voice forever calling on the——

1st Old Man [*frenziedly*]. No name, no name, man !

2nd Old Man. To go away.

1st Old Man. There in the sad innocence of day, stood the figuro of the laddo weaving a fountain outa him in a way that was a menace to morality ; with thousands of women, old, middle-aged, and young sthruggling to get a close-up view. I had to fight a way outa the crowd, with them clawing at me clothes so that a decent habiliment become a thing o' shreds and patches.

[*Two men, arm in arm, come in ; one is deaf, the other is blind. The blind one is wearing thick, dark glasses that, masklike, cover more than half his face. Both wear tall-hats, one light grey, the other, black ; one wears a coat with tails, the other a dinner-jacket ; one wears red trousers, the other green ones. Both sport collars and ties. The blind one carrying a natty walking-stick. They come to the centre, one looking back towards the houses, the other*

B.G.C.——H

*looking frontways.   Both of them seem to be in something
of a flutter.   They are linked together in a reverse way so
that they have to walk in a revolving manner, and, when
they stop, each looks forward in a reverse way to the
other.*

Blind Man to Old Men. What's going on in the city's
centre ? Didyas hear ?

Deaf Man turning to face Old Men. Didyas see ? I'm a
Reporter from the *Irish Horn* and me friend's one from
the *Dublin Flute.* I tell him what I sees. He tells me
all he hears, God help us. We asked lots o' torn and
tattered men staggering home what it was, but all
they'd say was Figuro, Figuro.

2nd Old Man. A Figuro plumb in the centre of O'Connell
Street where the bowl of light used to be ; a Figuro of
a more impudent, sturdier——

1st Old Man. And handsomer——

2nd Old Man. Figuro of a Peter Pan cascading conse-
quential shame and disgrace on all beholders.

1st Old Man. Forming a scintillatin', circular, set-in
fountain around himself, constantly expanding, the
younger girls, strong enough to force a way to the front,
sans stockings and shoes, and skirts, paddling gay in it,
all chanting together, Behold, Them who were lost
have been found, and them who were dead have come
to life again ! Each of them sing, singing solemnly,
       If I was th' only girl in th' world,
       An' you were the only boy.

Blind Man. When we heard the rumour, we guessed it
was a hydrogen bomb.

2nd Old Man. Would to the good God it was only such an innocent thing !

[*The Blind Man whispers into the Deaf Man's ear.*]

Deaf Man. Good God ! And what are our Civic Guards doing ?

1st Old Man. They're there and they aren't there.

2nd Old Man. You see, the women, young and old, thousands of them, trying to get close to the Figuro to catch a full glimpse of its intimations, pulled them down, overpowered them, misadjusted their uniforms, and endangered the unfortunate men's erectitude of feelin's.

1st Old Man. Near desthroyed them, but not a one of them yielded.

Young Man. And damned sorry a lot of them are they didn't, for all things was set ajinglin' !

2nd Old Man [*Jingle bells*]. For God's sake, don't give in now, Jimmy.

1st Old Man. The women were too many for the Civic Guards, and started scratching, biting, and kicking, when the Guards tried to drag them from their doom of undoing, so the Guards had to go, and now they're up on the roofs of the buildings appealing to the women to form a queue.

2nd Old Man. And the women who couldn't get close, ran into the higher buildings, up the stairs, and made for the windas to get a bird's-eye view of the Figuro's

———

1st Old Man. No name, no name, Mr. Tynan.

2nd Old Man. Figuro's Peek-a-boo. Darkness has come upon the Light of Other Days.

1st Old Man. The Fire Brigade hurried up, too, to help.

Young Man. Yes, and what did they do ? Shoved their long ladder out over the heads of the women, and fought like hell among themselves to be the first to climb out and garland their vision with Oh, the Sight Enthrancing !

Blind Man. Oh, Quid nunc pro quo ! What a thing it is not to be able to see a thing !

Deaf Man [*pitifully*]. Oh, Kay ! Oh, Kay ! What a calamity not to be able to hear a jingle !

2nd Old Man. There was the Legion of Mary wailing their prime right to be let go to the front to form a poster-ring of protection to prevent anyone wearing a skirt from seeing what would demolish every idea in every girlish heart to ever again carry a cross for Ireland.

Young Man. They should let the girls look at it long enough to tire of it, I say.

2nd Old Man. Jimmy, Jimmy, what if they never tired of it ? What in God's name are you thinking of ? Are yeh listening ?

Young Man. Y' heard me. I heard you. Let us alone, and we'll soon see how foolish it is to press and push and probe to squint at a taciturnal activity sorting us out away from what we often think we are.

    [*The cry of many crows is heard, intermingling with the loud hooting of many owls. They all look upwards as the cries go on.*

1st Old Man. Hear that, hear them ? There's all kinds of evil things flitting about. Oh who'll call for th' robin an' th' wren ! Do try to realise, Jimmy, lad, what we're all facin'. The unholy figaries of this Figuro is doing all an evil thing can with its bellycose sinuosities to set the souls of young men and young girls jockeying together away from where they are to the point of no return.

2nd Old Man. And the vibrations, Michael Murphy — remember ?

1st Old Man. God between us and them ! When the girls got anywhere near, and Figuro seen they had seen it, how the instrument he was handling shot up and down in stretched dimensions.

2nd Old Man. At the mid hour o' night when stars were weepin', the vibrations making the sky above open and shut like a shuttle, sending the clouds into a mad tangle of twisting trepidation, the old men and the Civic Guards shouting The End Is Come !

1st Old Man. And the girls and young men shouting The Beginning Is Here !

2nd Old Man. And thousands of Guardian Angels, beset with sudden anxiety, rushing woefully hitherwards and thitherwards, searching for missing souls, chanting frantically, Where, oh where is me wandering child tonight !

1st Old Man. Where, oh where can it be ! [*Overhead and round about are heard the frantic coo-coos of many cuckoos, the rasping rattles of many corncrakes, and the croaks of many ravens. Those who hear listen in silence till the sounds fade away.*] Hear them ? Bad signs, them. [*In the distance is heard a slow rumbling peal of thunder.*] And thunders, too !

2nd Old Man [*to the Young Man*]: See, son ? Understand now ? We all have to stand fast, immovable, against letting this Figuro of the Night devastate and desthroy forever the chastity of Ireland that for so long and so often has dizzied and dazzled the whole breathless world !

Blind Man. But what're yous going to do about it — that's the point ?

2nd Old Man [*to the Young Man — ignoring the question*]. Savvy, don't you, son ? If our poor modest-minded girls lie down under this Figuro — and they're doing it, mind you, already — and the young men refuse to mount guard over them to protect them from the evil of the foggy dew, then Ireland and her virtue is a gonner !

Deaf Man. What're yous all saying ?
          [*The Blind Man whispers into the Deaf Man's ear.*

1st Old Man. A gonner ! Understand, my lad ? Think ! You want to keep your infra-ray emotions closed up in cold storage ; no letting loose ; buttoned up to the chin, my lad.

2nd Old Man. Whenever you diagnose any suspicious feeling risin' up, check it firmly, at once ; don't hesitate. Say stoutly with heart and mind, This Sort of Thing Will Have to Stop !

Blind Man. Yous are wasting time ! Why don't yous take prompt action to restore law and ordher ?

1st Old Man [*ignoring the Blind Man — to the Young Man*].
See the danger, my lad ?   Listen, all : I seen a Star of
the County Down making for an upright young Civic
Guard, and before the unfortunate fella could dodge
her, her little hand got a grip on a shoulder. I heard
him yell ; then I glimpsed him flying by me, hell-bent
for the nearest hospital, his shoulder blacken'd and
burn'd to the bone, his arm blazin' ! It was a dreadful
sight ; but he didn't yield, he didn't give in to her !

2nd Old Man. I seen worse ; I seen one who did.

1st Old Man. Worse ? Tell us it then, Mr. Tynan.

2nd Old Man. I seen hellzapoppin in and out of the soul
of a saucy girl and out of a soul of a Civic Guard
surrendering ; I did that same !

Blind Man. Tell us it then, and God help us to hear and
profit.
                    [*The Deaf Man takes notes in a tiny book.*

2nd Old Man. After being beaten and battled outa the
crowd, and me sitting down on the railings outsidea the
Bank of Ireland, bemoaning me condition of tatterment,
me heart whirring round inside me like a dynamo gone
outa control, all the time thinking far within me would
I or would I not ever return to the time-beat of contentment of a tantamount life again.

1st Old Man [*impatiently*]. Yes, yes, we know ; tell all
you seen, and don't keep us consthraining ourselves !

2nd Old Man. I seen Kathleen Mavoorneen sailing
straight for a gossoon of a Civic Guard, and he standing
gaping at her condescendin' bodice slipping, slipping
down lower and lower, his innocent mouth open, eyes

a-poppin', helpless ; waiting to be coddled be the sin
ablaze in her ; then she whipt him into her arms, and
then I saw them gone, leaving only two red flames
twisting round one another !

1st Old Man. Two flames ! Red flames, mind yous !

2nd Old Man. That lepped up, then died down, blinding
me, and the last I seen of the pair was two tiny puffs
o' smoke twirling round each other, making for the
clouds high over Nelson's Pillar — all that was left of
honour and truth and stainless youth of a gallant Gael
and Girl of Ireland !

1st Old Man [*to the Young Man*]. Hear that, son ? Two
little wisps o' smoke.

Blind Man. Black or white smoke ? That's important.

2nd Old Man. Black as hell ! But wait a minute —
telling it even frightens me.
                              [*He covers his face with his hands.*

1st Old Man [*impatiently*]. Go on, go on, man ; let's hear
the worst !

2nd Old Man. Suddenly outa the puffs o' smoke, a little
owl and a littler one shot out and down towards the
earth.

Blind Man. White owls or black ? That's important.

2nd Old Man. White they were till near the solid earth,
then suddenly they became black as the smoke they
came from ; down they came. They came shooting
down !

1st Old Man. Hootin' ?

2nd Old Man. Shrill and sad. They touched the road a few yards from where I sat ; touched, and went through ; went through the solid earth without a sound bar a shriller shootin' hoot !

Young Man [*in an outburst*]. I don't believe a god-damned word of it !

1st Old Man. Jimmy, what're you saying ? You can't deny the proof given here, this very minute, of a young lad lost be a look at a handsome hussy's bodice slipping away from her bonnie breasts.

2nd Old Man. What are you saying, Michael Murphy ? Realise, man, that you are provokin' dangerous thoughts in a young and heedless head !

Young Man. It's not the first time they were mentioned. I know a Gaelic song that sings of the delight of the snowy breasts of a true love. How could he ha' known they were white as snow, if she hadn't shown them to him ?

2nd Old Man. See, Mr. Murphy ? Your careless blather is doing great harm.

Young Man. I'll sing the song to show yous I'm right, so I will.

Blind Man. We want no song o' that kind sung here, boy.

Young Man. How would yous know what it was saying, anyhow, since yous don't know the Gaelic ?

1st Old Man. The sound o' the syllables 'ud tell us what we didn't want to know !

Young Man. Why not a little alarm about yourselves, seeing your souls enclose nothing but a tatthered roguery? I seen yous in the crowd clutching at any girl near yous, shouting for help when a lass bowled yous over and hopped away without waiting to see where yous fell.

1st Old Man. Hear that, Mr. Tynan?

2nd Old Man. He's just misconsthruin' things.

Young Man. Every living thing goes in couples, so why shouldn't lads and lasses do the same?

2nd Old Man. Oh, Lord, oh, Lord!

1st Old Man. Whisht, lad! It's a sad thing and not a thrue one to make out that two God-fearin' mortals would be, could be, affected be any display of silk-sinisthered legs!

2nd Old Man [*anguished*]. Silk-sinisthered legs! [*Shouting*] I'm tellin' you, you're registherin' evil ideas inta th' middle o' th' young man's mind!

Young Man. I seen yous, me holy buckoes, groping and rowdying about in the spare parts of the crowd, looking for what you couldn't get even if you got it!

Blind Man. Ordher, ordher; this discussion is exceeding the limits of decent and respectable controversy.

Deaf Man. What th' hell are yous all blatherin' about?

Young Man. Why did God make girls as they are and laddies as they are, if He didn't want them to get together — Answer me that!

Blind Man [*burying his face in his hands*]. Jasus! This is terrible!

Deaf Man. Let's go.   No use of staying here — I can't hear a damned word.

[*A form slides in from the back of the houses, a slim form of a young lad with more than a touch of a bird in his look. He is all in black — black narrow trousers, close-fitting black jersey.   The legs of the trousers don't come right down, and it is seen that he is wearing bright yellow socks and yellow sandals or shoes.   He carries a tight- fitting green cap on his head with a peak projecting out and pointed like the beak of a bird.   Indeed, he would look very much like a crow, but for the green cap on his head.   He comes in chuckling that sounds something like the caw of a crow too.   When he speaks, his voice sounds the words with the burr of a caw on each or some of them.*

Birdlike Lad [*with a gay cawing laugh*]. It's springing up everywhere !   In Cork yesterday, in Limerick today, in Galway tomorrow, in Sligo the day after.   [*He laughs in a crowlike way.*]   Caw Caw Caw Caw !

1st Old Man. Who are you ?   What are you trying to say ?

Birdlike Lad. Figuro is an abounding joy everywhere at last.

2nd Old Man. Cork, Limerick, Galway, and Sligo !   I want to know what the bishops are doing ?   Why don't they get a move on ?   Why don't they get croaking ?

Birdlike Lad. The Bishops are seated at a Round Table in the Senate Room, Maynooth, powerless — they can do nothing but join in Community singing.

1st Old Man. Community singin' at this time !   Com- munity hymn singin', is it ?

Birdlike Lad. No ; songs.

2nd Old Man. Sacred or Profane songs ? What sorta songs ?

Birdlike Lad. Love songs. They've already sung ' Coming thro' th' Rye ' ; ' Diaphenia's like th' Daffodown-dilly ' ; [*He gestures silence.*] Whisht ! I can hear them singing now, full-voiced, ' Come and Kiss Me, Sweet and Twenty '.

1st Old Man [*sinking down*]. They've got th' touch ; they're undher a spell !

Blind Man. They've become ambivalent ; they're no longer expertise ; they've demoted themselves. They've commuted from God to man !

Deaf Man. What's bein' said ? [*Blind Man whispers to him.*] Oh God ! It's the Last Post ; the lights are going out in Ireland !

Young Man [*rejoicing*]. Th' old lights, an' time, too ! New lights for old !

2nd Old Man [*vehemently*]. Something must be done !

1st Old Man. An' at oncest !

Blind Man. Something must be done, somehow, some-where, sometime. Can neither of yous think of nothing !

2nd Old Man [*violently — to Blind — and Deaf Man*]. You, yous damned idle-minds, coddin' as Irish with your wisply words, think of something yourselves, other than what people tell to yous !

1st Old Man. Calm, Mr. Tynan, calm. We must keep together.

Young Man [*suddenly and vehemently*]. To hell with the lot
o' yous — I'm for the thrust and throe of Figuro !
[*He goes over to the house where the Girl is, and calls up.*]
Alice, where art thou ?

2nd Old Man. Wait a second, don't give in yet ! There's
one power that stands undaunted still !

1st Old Man [*testily*]. Well, tell us, tell us, man, what
power stands undaunted still !

2nd Old Man. Can you think of nothing, eediot ? [*He
gets to his feet excitedly.*] The North, man, the North !
The Northern iron and the steel will smash Figuro
into bits !

Birdlike Lad [*with a cawing laugh of derision*]. The North ?
Bah, you bastards, Figuro is in Belfast, too, and he is
also on his way to Portadown !

Blind Man. Belfast !

1st Old Man. Portadown, too !

2nd Old Man [*sinking down again — utterly dejected*]. We're
bet, Mr. Murphy ; we're finished, Mr. Murphy ; this
is the end !

Birdlike Lad [*to Blind Man and Deaf Man ; while he speaks his
words are accompanied by, not loud but clear, hoots of owls,
caws from rooks, and rattles from corncrakes*]. Off you go,
the pair of you, to your airless little office, to write
your scraps of gossip, and try to tell your shrinking
little world that the world outside is changing.
[*They go out slowly, backwards, before him, arm in arm as
they came in ; stopping now and then as if to resist, but
slowly retreating before the Birdlike Lad till they disappear. While they are slowly going, the Young Man,*]

looking up at the window out of which the Young Girl
looked, sings his appeal to her to open the door and let him
in ; having first taken a bunch of bright blue ribbons
from a breast pocket. He looks up as the Young Girl
appears at the window.

Young Man [*singing up to her*] :
    Sweet Alice, I've brought you th' blue ribbons,
    For long in our country so rare ;
    So open th' door, an' then dare me
    To tie up your bonnie brown hair !
  [*The Young Girl appears at window. She is wearing a*
  silver bodice.

1st Old Man [*pointing up at her*]. The silver apples of the
moon !

Young Girl [*singing*] :
    You've brought me th' bonnie blue ribbons,
    So lovely, so rich, an' so fair ;
    So I'll open th' door, an' then dare you
    To tie up my bonnie brown hair !
  [*She goes from the window, and after a moment, opens the*
  door, catches his hand, and draws him into the house,
  closing the door when he has gone in. She is now
  dressed in blue skirt and sparkling silver bodice.

1st Old Man ⎱ [*together*]. ⎰ She'll do for him, now !
2nd Old Man ⎰   ⎱ He'll do for her, now !
  [*The music of a dance begins, and the Old Men cock their*
  ears to listen.

1st Old Man. They're creepin' in on us, Mr. Tynan.

2nd Old Man. They'll soon be on top of us in earnest, Mr.
Murphy !

2nd Old Man. Better me to be lyin' stiff an' cold under this Sacred Memorial here, ere this thing happened.

1st Old Man. An me below, an' deep below, th' Cross I'm claspin'.

> [*As the Old Men are speaking, young girls and lads come in dancing. The lads are brightly dressed, one in a green coat, one in a red, another in a coat of deep orange hue, still another in a royal-blue one ; the girls are in white, grey, brown, or black, but each one carries a bow of brilliant blue ribbons in her hair.*

> [*After they have danced a little while, the Young Girl comes out, in her blue skirt and silver bodice, with the Young Man, who is now wearing blue trousers and a golden coat. The dancers pause to let them join in.*

2nd Old Man [*pointing at Young Man's golden coat*]. Th' golden apples of th' sun !

> [*The Old Men sink down, one clasping the Obelisk, the other clasping the Cross while the couples dance around them — gay and hopeful. The dance quickens, while voices at a distance sing ' He Promised to Buy Me a Bunch of Blue Ribbons '. The Dance continues as the Curtain falls.*

> *Note : The Dance of the Young People should be partly processional. Maybe Chopin's celebrated Polonaise in A would do fine.*

THE MOON SHINES ON
KYLENAMOE

Just above the distant green mountains, the pale moon is shining, giving a quiet silence to the valley of Kylenamoe in the County of Melloe. It is just on midnight and here within the fifteen or so houses forming the village in the valley, all life is sleeping, the moon housing all the quiet homes there within a gentle lullaby light. Even the lover and his lass, if such there ever be on road, boreen, or field-path, in the village of Kylenamoe, had gone away from active service, and no further life would come to light till the sun of a new morning rose again — or, so it seemed. The place is what the residents of Kylenamoe call a Railway Station, but there is only one train stopping in the early morning, and one, once in a while, stopping there at night, though many more whirl through it during the day, and several goods trains rumble through during the night, hardly knowing that they pass through a Railway Station. The actual little landing-place, called a Platform, is off to the right, for the railway line passes by off to the right, parallel to the side of the village, now sleeping a mile or two away to the left. Not quite all are within the arms of sleep; no, not quite all. To the left of the visible scene is a hut, called the Goods Store, but it also holds the lanterns for the signal, the oil, the waste with which to clean them, and any odd tool that may be used on the Station — a brush, and a truck with which to wheel any heavy goods that may be brought once in a while to the farmers of the surrounding district, or the goods that occasionally come to furnish out the little General Store that supplies the immediate and daily needs of the village people. To the right of this hut, a little way to the rear, the signal stands about three or four feet above the roof, rising to the cross-blade painted white, with a black thick stroke down its middle; on the reverse, painted red with a white panel perpendicularly traversing the

125

middle of it ; at the side are the movable coloured slides, one red, the other green, which when placed before the lighted lantern throw a red or a green light a good distance, telling an engine-driver whether to halt, when it shows red, or to go on, when it shows green. At present, the signal is showing a green light. The signalman reaches them by going up an iron ladder attached to the standard, to fit the lantern in its bed. A ladder leads to the upper storey of the hut, and here there is a hand-lever at the butt of the signal-standard which enables him to switch a point on any rare occasion.

To the right is a small cottage with a thatched roof ; only part of it can be seen showing a tiny window which allows only a protrusion of head and shoulders, and a narrow door, its step leading into the room (for the floor is below ground level) almost covered with coarse grass. It is the home of an old fellow of near 70, Corny, and his wife, Martha. He works still as a railway labourer on a length of the railway-line, and has done so for over fifty years now.

Sean Tomasheen comes in from the left, wearing a thick muffler round his neck ; an official railway peaked cap, circled by a wide green band ; corduroy trousers, and a reddish-grey coat. He is a young man of 24 or 25 years old ; not bad-looking, but rather thin, tall, and a little ungainly. He is softly singing the well-known song from The Bohemian Girl — *' I Dreamt that I Dwelt in Marble Halls'. He climbs the ladder-steps to the upper storey of the hut, and, after a moment, the signal-light which has been at green changes to red. He appears again, descends the ladder, gazes out intently to the right, then goes into the lower part of the hut and comes out with a truck built to carry little more than two or three cwts. He stands the truck upright, leaning and holding one of its shafts, gazing all the time towards the right.*

After a moment, he lilts the song he has been singing :

I dreamt that I dwelt in marble halls,

With vassals and serfs at me side,
And of all who assembled within those walls,
That I was th' hope and th' pride.

*The distant whistle of a train is heard, followed shortly after
by the sound of its coming. Sean Tomasheen immediately
becomes alert, he grips the two shafts of the truck, and faces it
towards the right, evidently waiting for the coming train. The
song tails away into silence.*

I had riches too great to count — could boast
Of . . . a . . . high, ancesthral . . . name.

*The train has slid into the Halt ; we heard it coming
louder and louder, and then into quietness as it halted before
reaching the Red Light. Sean Tomasheen hurries out with the
truck, and in a few short moments comes back pushing it towards
the hut, having on it a sack or two, a bale, and a box. He is
followed by the Guard who is dressed in dark-blue uniform, and
wears a peaked cap similar to Sean's, but the Guard's is circled
by a band of silver ; he carries some dockets in his hand.*

Guard. Bag o' phosphates for Dermody, sack o' cattle-
feed for Ballantine's General Stores, a box for the
Honourable Jeremy Erskine — who's he ?

Sean. One o' th' lawdee daws, I suppose, brightenin' be
his presence th' Manor House o' Kilnagappell, away
beyant the Ballantines' place behind the Hill o' th'
Heather.

Guard. Huh. Well, make it snappy, Sean ; can't waste
time ; ten minutes behind already, lad.

Sean. No passengers this time ?

Guard. This time ! An' when did you or me or anyone
else ever see a passenger hoppin' out of a thrain goin' up

or one comin' down to plant a Christian or a heathen foot on th' holy soil of Kylenamoe ?

Sean [*as he drops the shafts of the truck by the door of the hut, and takes the dockets from the Guard to sign them*]. Me, no ; but others may have.

Guard. An' what others, may I ask ? An' when ? An' why ? ay, an' whither, too ?

Sean. You never know. One o' these fine days someone or other may get a notion, an' disperse herself or himself into seein' what kinda place Kylenamoe is.

Guard [*as he takes the signed dockets from Sean*]. You can see what you want to see from a safe distance. Well, I must be goin'. We're ten minutes behind already.

Sean [*who has glanced off right — excitedly*]. Looka, looka !

Guard. Be God, a passenger ! It can't be ! What carriage did he get outa ? Must be mistakin' th' stop. Comic-lookin' guy. Is it a real guy someone dumped there for a joke ? [*As the two gape to the right.*] It's movin' ; it's a livin' thing, right enough. Carryin' an umbrella in one paw an' an attaché case in t'other. What'll be done with this guy, for he must be well out of his mind !

Sean. Looka th' way th' thing's dhressed ! Where can he be goin' ? Is he walkin' in his sleep or wha' ? What landed him here, I wondher ? Maybe he's one o' them guys that go out catchin' butterflies.

Guard. You don't catch butterflies this time o' night, man ! Looks a sinisther figure to me.

Sean [*thoughtfully*]. He has a prowl of a look about him right enough, if y'know what I mean.

Guard. Yis.   Menacin', too, I'd say.   You never know.
Someone ought to keep an eye on him.

Sean. Won't be me.   [*In a half-whisper.*]   Looka, he's
comin' towards us.

Guard [*swiftly turning away his head and looking towards the
hut*].   Turn your gob away, man !   Don't let him see
you gapin' !   Keep your head down :   we're busy with
th' dockets.
>   [*They bend over the dockets as Lord Leslieson of Ottery St.
>   Oswald comes in from the right.   He does look a curious
>   figure, dressed up to guard against the night air.   He
>   wears the cap one sees in pictures worn by skiers, thick
>   wool, coloured, and pulled down over brow and ears ;
>   a thick cape-like coat falling to his knees, and when the
>   flaps divide, we see that he is wearing plus-fours, with
>   gaudy-coloured stockings ;   to finish up, he has a thick,
>   long, woollen muffler of blue and yellow around his neck,
>   the ends falling over his shoulders, and flowing down his
>   back ;   and to finish down, he wears a pair of thick-soled
>   brogues.   He carries an attaché case and an umbrella.   He
>   is sure of himself, utterly unconscious of his comic aspect ;
>   confident of his position and importance, and quite at his
>   ease as the men of his place in society usually are.   He
>   comes over to the two men, and taps the Guard on the back.*

Lord Leslieson. I say, gentlemen, would you tell me the
way out, please ?

Guard [*turning around*].   Way out ?

Sean. You're in th' way out just as you're in th' way in,
sir.

L. Leslieson [*a bit puzzled*].   Eh ?   Oh, I mean the way out
or the way into Kylenamoe.

Guard. You couldn't be in it more'n y'are.   Right here you're right there.

L. Leslieson [*more puzzled*]. Eh ?   Oh, I see — the Irish way of joking. [*He gives a feeble laugh.*] Heh heh heh ! What I wish, gentlemen, is to be directed to Kyle-namoe.

Guard. You're there, I'm tellin' you.

L. Leslieson. The town, sir ; the town.

Guard. What town have you got in your mind, sir ?

L. Leslieson. The town of Kylenamoe, of course.

Sean. Town is it ? [*Sweeping his arms around in a circle.*] This whole expanse is th' town. [*To the Guard*] Isn't it, Mick ?

Guard. Yis ; if yeh take it that way, it's the biggest town in th' land.

L. Leslieson. I beg you, gentlemen, no joking. I'm Lord Leslieson of——

[*As he says this, a shrill whistle comes from the engine out to the right, either a warning or a summoning blast.*

Sean [*to the Guard*]. There's your buttie engine-driver whisperin' you to come back, Mick.

Guard [*testily*]. I know — I heard him !

Sean. Well, aren't you goin' ?

Guard [*more testily still*]. I'll be goin' when I go ! That damned whistlin' laddo'll do harm yet sthrivin' to be before time. I'm told when he was a kid, he was always hurtin' himself runnin' to get in front of him-self !

Sean. You said a minute ago yourself, you were in a hurry.

Guard [*indignantly*]. I did not !

Sean [*vehemently*]. Yes, yeh did ! You were in such a sweat of a hurry you were nearly growin' wings to fly off when I was signin' th' dockets !

L. Leslieson [*agitatedly*]. Gentlemen, listen——

Guard [*indignantly — to Sean*]. Looka you, I know you of old goin' about scarifyin' th' thruth. I'm dealin' with a railway question, amn't I ? I'm thryin' to iron out th' difficulty of a customer, amn't I ? A first-class customer, too. [*Suddenly — to Lord Leslieson*] You thravelled first-class, didn't you ?

L. Leslieson. Of course, I did.

Guard [*to Sean*]. There, you see ! A first-class customer that wants to have a difficulty settled afther gettin' outa me thrain, an' I'm th' guard, amn't I ?

Sean. I know : you dhress like th' guard, you blather like th' guard, an' th' thrain's waitin' for you to start her ; so you ought to be th' guard.

Guard [*in a shout*]. I am th' guard !

L. Leslieson. Gentlemen, peace, please ! This discussion isn't helping me in the slightest degree. I am on an exceedingly important mission, gentlemen, which must be, must be, fulfilled tonight ; tonight, gentlemen.

Guard. Th' night is young, an' th' mornin's a long way off ; an' we're doin' all we can to help you. [*To Sean*] Aren't we, Sean Tomasheen ?

Sean. 'Course we are ! [*To Lord Leslieson*] Just you tell us where you want to go an' what you want us to do, sir.
[*Just as Lord Leslieson is about to tell them, the engine whistles again, this time shriller and longer than the whistle that sounded before. The Guard and Sean gape at each other while the whistle blows.*

Guard [*challengingly to Sean, after a pause*]. Were yeh goin' to say something ?

Sean. No, no ; [*he looks towards the right where the engine is, lifts his head a little to lilt more clearly, and sings the line*] : I hear you ca–ll–ing me–e–e !

Guard [*turning to Lord Leslieson*]. Hear that ? There's Kylenamoe for you !

L. Leslieson. Your friend didn't mean to be rude to you.

Guard. Me friend ! What he'd like is the silver band round his cap an' th' red one round mine. His whole insinuendo was fair seethin' with malice !

L. Leslieson. You can settle this dispute between yourselves later on. Please inform me of where I want to go and how to get there.

Sean. An' how th' hell can we tell yeh where yeh want to go if yeh can't tell where yeh want to go yourself ?

Guard. An' we'll settle our dispute when an' where we choose, too.

L. Leslieson. Please, gentlemen, don't misunderstand me. My remark meant no disrespect to your choice of place or time to settle your dispute, I assure you.

Guard. You can't sliddher off from your insultin' remark in that easy way, me bucko ! No use thryin' to back out of it now.

Sean [*emphatically*]. No, no damned use. [*To the Guard*] We savvy these blithe boyos flittin' over here to tell th' Irish off !

L. Leslieson. You give a wrong implication, sirs, to a perfectly innocent remark. Indeed, I'm so confused, I hardly know what I said.

Guard [*derisively*]. Oho, but bedamnit, that's a good one !

Sean [*derisively, too*]. Didn't hear what he was sayin'. Th' poor man !

Guard [*emphatically*]. We heard it, anyhow. [*Decisively — to Lord Leslieson*] You can't break through th' sound barrier here, me good man. A smile afther an insult can't alienate a denial.

Sean. We know, Mick : Hoof of a horse, horns of a bull, smile of an Englishman, eh ?

L. Leslieson. Please listen, friends——

Sean. Friends now — well, be God, that's better than a good one !

L. Leslieson. My one and only object in coming down to this desolate district was to carry out an urgent and a delicate mission.

Sean [*indignantly*]. Desolate ? What d'ye mean, desolate ? What's desolate about it ? There's houses here, there's people here, there's Callaghan's Stores only five or so miles away ; so how th' hell d'ye call it desolate ?

L. Leslieson [*more and more confused*]. Oh, no, no ; just a figure of speech, just a figure of speech, friends.

Guard. A damned odd figure of speech.

Sean. What d'ye mean, figure o' speech? Let's get to th' bottom of this——

Guard [*resentfully — to Sean*]. Aw, don't be thryin' to worry us with your silly questions — why he thinks Kylenamoe desolate an' what he really means be a figure of speech. Them's trivial things, an' th' way he's motionin' himself, he wouldn't be able to tell us anyhow.

Sean [*hotly*]. I don't see why Englishmen should be given leave to come down all th' way to Kylenamoe in ordher to vilify Ireland in th' very face of Irishmen themselves !

L. Leslieson [*patiently*]. My good man, I didn't vilify Ireland, and had no intention of doing so.

Sean. It sounded damned like it, for—— [*he suddenly stops, stretches out his arms so as to get them in front of Lord Leslieson and the Guard, waving them back a little as he steps back, too*] Jasus, will yous look at what's comin' towards us at this unholy time o' th' night !

Guard. Patrick Dunphy's boy an' Mave Linanawn, arms round each other, lost to th' world at large ! Musta been at a dance or somethin'.

Sean [*excitedly*]. There's no dance anywhere tonight, not one ; an' if there was, it would be in another direction altogether. What are they doin' here on railway property ? That pair has been up to no good.

Guard. What else, an' they stealin' evil excitements within th' secret niches of th' night.

Sean. All sense o' decency hidden away from th' undulations of forbidden thoughts.

L. Leslieson [*impatiently*]. Oh, nonsense ! For heaven's sake, let's confine our attention to the problem of my getting where I want to go. [*Indicating with a gesture towards where the couple are.*] This is no unusual sight, men. Just another lover and his lass. They are to be seen everywhere.

Guard. What, in Kylenamoe ?

Sean. At this time o' th' night ?

L. Leslieson [*losing his patience — loudly, almost a shout*]. At any time of the night, fool !

Sean [*to the Guard*]. Hear that, Mick !

Guard [*seriously*]. In your counthry, yessir ; not here ; so th' sooner you get back there, th' betther an' safer for us !

L. Leslieson [*still angry*]. I'm not interested in your Dunphy's boy or the girl he's hooking with his arm. [*Explosively*] I want to get to the town !
   [*As he speaks the young man and his lass come in, each with an arm around the other, seeing nothing except themselves as they gaze lovingly and sentimentally into each other's face.*]

Boy. Gra mo chree, I'd rather own you than own all Ireland, without division ; I would, achisleh !

Girl. Yis, I know, aroon ; but would you rather own me than any other girl o' the village ?

Sean [*coming briskly and indignantly towards the couple*]. What're ye doin' here, eh ? What're ye doin' anywhere on the open road at this time o' th' night, eh ?

Boy. That's none of your business.

Sean. It's my business till I report your conduct to th' priest, first thing in th' mornin'.

Girl. It's a comfort anyway, Tommysheen, that you haven't to report it last thing at night.

Sean [*indignantly*]. Cocky, aren't yous ! D'ye know that yous are on private property, belongin' to th' railway ? Yous aren't allowed here.   Yous are threspassers, so yous are.   D'ye know it's half-way past midnight ?

Guard [*squinting at his watch*]. Twenty-five minutes to one it is.

Sean. Where were yous an' what were yous doin' ?

Boy [*his temper is rising*]. Are you, y'omadhaun, me father confessor, or what ?

Girl [*gently pulling him away*]. Thor leat, aw Fawdhrig. Let us go, let them tarry, let them sink or let them swim.

Sean. Get outa here, th' pair o' yez.   If anyone saw yez, a nice name th' place would get, an' me to be blamed for providin' it for yez.   Yous aren't passengers from th' thrain, are yous, like this gentleman here ?

L. Leslieson [*almost frantically*]. Oh, a truce to your stupid chattering, and let me speak.   Let this worthy couple go on their way, and without further molestation.   [*To the couple*] Go on, my dears, get a move on.

Boy [*resentfully*]. Who're you tellin' to get a move on, eh ?   Are you an Inspecthor of the Garda Sheehah-cawnah, or what ?

L. Leslieson [*in desperation*]. On, boy, on ! I don't know what I am this moment, or where I am, or what I'm doing !

Sean [*hotly and resentfully*]. You're in Kylenamoe — yeh know that much, don't you !

L. Leslieson. I want to hire a car to take me into the town.

Guard [*startled now*]. Hire a car !

Girl [*in wonderment*]. Town ?

Boy. Yerra, what town ?

L. Leslieson. I'm in a state, a condition, of utter confusion with so many questions to me, and the answers given to my questions — hopelessly confused !

Sean. You've tumbled yourself into a configuration of confusions be not knowin' where you're goin' or what yeh want to do.

L. Leslieson. I told you, I've told you — I'm on a mission !

Boy [*suddenly seeing the light*]. I know now — he's one o' them poker-faced Jehovah-Witness Missioners, or, maybe, a Mormon, come down here to thry to rattle us outa th' right way !

Girl [*defiantly*]. He'd better go back to where he came from !

L. Leslieson [*violently*]. No ! No, I tell you ! I'm not a gospeller ! I'm on a political mission ; I carry despatches for——
    [*Once more the engine whistles ; this time, three short, sharp whistles, insistent and imperative.*

Sean [*unable to resist the inclination, singing*] :
        I hear you ca–ll–ing me !

Guard. All th' pharmaceutical chemists of th' world couldn't mix a man into a bigger bastard than you, Tomasheen !

[*The door of the house on the right opens and Cornelius
Conroy appears there.   He is about 70, greyish-bearded.
He has a bed-quilt wrapped round him, an old cap
thrust back to front on his head, and his bare feet are
encased in big, rough boots, unlaced.   At the same time,
the window of the house above the door opens, and Martha
Conroy appears there, leaning as far as she can out of it so
as to see the group at the other end, and Cornelius below her,
on the door's threshold.   All that is seen of her is wrapped
up in a red shawl, draped over head, like a hood, showing
but part of her brow, her cheeks, and something of her
chin.   Her arms rest on the sill, and her hands hold the
shawl closely around her.   She looks the same age as her
husband, has many wrinkles, but her eyes are bright and
her voice is clear.*]

Corny [*violently*]. What th' hell's goin' on here !   What's
all this terrific ragin' an' shoutin' an' screamin' of
engines, rousin' quiet-bedded people into frightened
attention ?

Martha [*echoing her husband's last words*]. Quiet-bedded
people into frightened attention.   Yis.

Corny. Years an' years now, night after night, your
engine, Michael Mulehawn, came in, went out, without one whistle, without a whisper.

Martha. Without one whistle, without a whisper.

Corny. Slid in an' slid out without a murmur.

Martha. Slid in, slid out, without a murmur.

Corny. Now Christian sleep is shatthered in a wild
calamity of noises !

Martha [*nodding her head violently*]. Calamity o' noises !

Sean. This gazebo [*indicating Lord Leslieson*] here's th' cause of it all.

Guard. We're labourin' to find out from him where he wants to go.

L. Leslieson [*indignantly*]. This is a slander ! I made it perfectly clear to all where I wanted to go. [*Pushing those away who may be in front of him, and hastening to stand in front of Cornelius.*] My good man, I simply am anxious to be directed to the, the town . . . town of . . . of . . . [*Unhappily*] Oh, with all the confusion of idiotic chatter, arguments, and disputes, I've forgotten the very name of the place !

Guard
Sean } [*together*]. Kylenamoe !

L. Leslieson [*standing in the middle of all, his arms gesticulating*]. I want to be directed without delay to the town of Kylenamoe !

Corny. Th' town ?

Martha [*echoing him*]. Town ?

Corny. Let's get it clear : Who is he, anyway ?

Martha [*leaning more forward out of the window*]. Speak up, man !

L. Leslieson. I'm Lord Leslieson of Ottery St. Oswald.

Guard. Never heard of him.

Corny. Nor me.

Martha. Never heard such a name whispered on the Four Winds of Eireann.

B.G.C.—K

Sean. Of all th' saints I heard tell of, I never heard of an Otthery St. Oswald mentioned ; not once.

L. Leslieson. I must speak to someone in authority. Where's your nearest telephone ?

Sean. Away in the Post Office.

L. Leslieson. Take me there at once, sir !

Sean. Whatja take me for — an' leave me important duties here an' goods as well to wait misfortune ?

Boy. Anyway, th' Post Office is dark, locked up, an' empty at this time o' th' night.

L. Leslieson [*jumping up on top of the box on the truck to add importance to what he is saying*]. Listen, people ; please listen ; carefully, and with all your attention. What I have to tell you is of vital importance. Understand that, please.

Guard [*impatiently*]. Get on with it, get on with it — don't be beatin' about th' bush !

Martha [*musingly, but clearly*]. He looks a wee bit flighty to me.

L. Leslieson. I carry important despatches for the Prime Minister of England, the Earl of Epplepen, holidaying somewhere here in the Manor House of Killnalayna. [*Hurriedly glances in a notebook taken from his pocket.*] I was instructed to fly to Dublin, take train from there in a reserved carriage, so that no one could engage me in conversation.

Corny [*ejaculating*]. Th' English again !

Martha [*echoing*]. English again !

L. Leslieson [*angrily — to Corny*]. Don't interrupt, man ! I was instructed to get out at Kylenamoe, hire a car, and hurry off to Killnalayna Manor. Now, get me a car without further aggravating argument, please !

   [*Andy O'Hurrie, the engine-driver, appears round the corner of Corny's house ; a short, stout man of 45 or so ; his face stained with oil and the blown-about specks of coal-dust ; red-faced, and wearing a close-cropped moustache. He is dressed in soiled dungarees, and holds a lump of oily waste in his hand. Anger stares from his face.*

Andy [*loudly and angrily*]. What th' hell ! Are we puttin' up here for th' night, or wha' ? Are yous organisin' an oul'-age kindergarten, or wha' ? D'ye know, Michael Mulehawn, that th' thrain has gone inta a doze waitin' for yeh ? What am I to say in me report when I get to me journey's end half an hour late, an' maybe an hour ?

L. Leslieson [*getting down from standing on top of the box, sitting down on it despairingly instead, elbows on his knees, and his face hidden in his hands*]. Another one of them !

Sean [*indicating Lord Leslieson*]. Fella sittin' on th' box is to blame for it.

Andy. What's he want ; who is he ?

Sean [*touching Lord Leslieson on his shoulder*]. Andy O'Hurrie wants to know who you are.

L. Leslieson [*with a moan*]. I'm Lord Leslieson of Ottery St. Oswald.

Corny [*repeating information*]. Lord Leslieson of Otthery St. Oswald.

Martha [*echoing*]. Otthery St. Oswald.

Andy. Is that so ?

Guard. He wants to get to the town.

Andy [*coming over to the group*]. Town ?   What town ?

Sean. Town o' Kylenamoe.

Andy [*with a touch of sympathy*]. Someoné musta been pullin' his leg.

L. Leslieson [*impatiently — sitting up sharply to answer Andy*]. Nonsense !   No Official at the Foreign Office would dare try to pull Lord Leslieson's leg.   Go back to your engine, man, if you wish to act the fool !

Andy [*indignantly*].   Who're you ordherin' about ?   Things is comin' to a nice pass if lord or lady comes down here all th' way from London to ordher a man about !   On th' engine, near th' engine, away from th' engine, within sight or outa sight of her is a matther to be instituted within me own personal investigation, an' altogether divided from any interloper's jurisdiction !

Guard [*to Lord Leslieson*]. You'd do well, me lord, to remember that the push of your hand or the back of your finger hasn't any power or status in Ireland now.

L. Leslieson [*sinking back on the box in his dejected aspect*]. All right, all right.   I know.

Boy. Comin' over here thinkin' th' ould power of keepin' us down was still performin' !

Sean [*turning angrily on the young couple*]. In th' sthress of our problem, I forgot yous two was still here !   Loitherin' about in th' nakedness o' th' night !   [*Solemnly*] We're not goin' to have our unsuspected names shuffled into any noddin' encouragement to your

rambles through th' randy dews on th' fondlin' fingers
of th' middle night-time !

Martha [*in a semi-squeal from the window*]. Yis ! Take
yourselves off, yeh fiddlers with temptations ! Home
with the pair o' yous ; an' hide yourselves from decent
people under th' clothes of your separate beds !

Girl [*pulling the Boy by the sleeve to get him to come*]. Come
on, agrah ; we've miles to go. Let us leave these fools
for God to help them ! [*They go out, each with an arm
around the other.*]

Sean [*as they go out*]. An' take your arms asundher from
around one another — we don't want anything un-
foreseen to happen here !

Corny. Whew ! Their goin' is a relief.

Martha. Their goin's a great relief.

Andy. Now th' counthry's cleared, yous had bctther bend
yourselves to gettin' this laddo to where he wants to go.

Sean [*shaking Lord Leslieson's shoulder gently*]. Eh, you, sit
up, an' fire away, an' tell us all in common-clear
manner exactly where yeh want to go, an' how you're
goin' to get there.

L. Leslieson [*impatiently*]. I've told you — Killnalayna
Manor, and I need a car to bring me there.

Sean [*aghast*]. A car !

Guard. What kind of a car ?

L. Leslieson. A motor car, a motor car.

Corny [*almost frightened*]. A motor car !

Martha [*echoing*]. Motor car !

L. Leslieson. That's why I want to get to the town — to hire one.

Andy. Th' town !

Corny. Yerra, what town ?

Martha. Town ? I said he looked a wee bit flighty !

Sean. This here, and thirty houses a mile away, fourteen of them empty.

L. Leslieson. But there must be one car among the inhabitants ?

Sean. Man alive, th' lot o' them, man an' woman, if not there already, is on th' tip o' 70. Car ! I dunno if one o' them has ever seen one, even from a distance. Neither kid nor car !

Guard. What about Corny there ?

Corny [*astonished*]. Me ?

Guard [*persuasively*]. At a pinch, now, an' considherin' th' disthress th' laddo is in, Jinnie could make th' road, an' dump him at his rendeevoo.

Corny. Jinnie ? At this hour o' th' night ?

Sean. Jinnie could do it, hands down. She's often gone there, an' knows every step o' th' way, an' would carry him gently along in her own sweet little way.

L. Leslieson [*who has raised his bent head to listen suspiciously to what is being said*]. What Jinnie ?

Sean [*reassuringly*]. Take no fear, sir. She isn't a mettlesome lass at all. She wouldn't bring you into any harm. Your journey would be just a lullaby.

L. Leslieson. Will you all please understand that I am an
Official of the English Foreign Office, a most important
person who cannot go gadding about lonely roads in
the hush of the night with any Jane or Jinnie !

Martha [*combatively from the window*]. Whatja mean, Janes
an' Jinnies gaddin' about on lonely roads in th' hush
o' th' night ? It's your dirty English mind thryin'
to prosthrate us ! Mr. Cornelius Conroy an' Mrs.
Martha Conroy, Mr. Cornelius Conroy's wife, has a
respectability throughout the four seasons of th' years
of a natural life is such as never once forced a single
dtch dtch from th' lips of th' holiest priest in Ireland !

Guard. Yous are all confusin' th' gentleman with your
Janes an' your Jinnies. [*To Lord Leslieson*] Looka, sir,
th' Jinnie specified isn't a skirt ; it's a dapper-wee
donkey that Corney uses in a creel-cart to bring turf
from th' bog, an' carry an odd bunch o' vegetation, an
odd hen or two, an' maybe a pig to an occasional
market. It's your one chance in this place, at this
night-hour, to struggle to where you want to go.

L. Leslieson [*aghast*]. What, stagger there in a turf creel-
cart pulled by a donkey !

Sean. With a wad o' sthraw undher your backside, snug
in th' creel-cart, you'd look like a Burren king on your
raygal seat. [*Unable to resist the humour of it, he lilts*] :
  Sweet chariot, comin' for to carry me home,
  Swe–et char–i–o–t, comin' for to carry me home !

L. Leslieson [*in a rage*]. No, sirs, no ! I know what you
Irish are like ! It would all be rushed into the Irish
papers : Important Official of the English Foreign
Office travels to the Prime Minister on a sod of turf in

a creel-car ! It would spread to our English Press, and I should become a mockery in my own country till the present generation died out, and I died with it !

Sean. It's your only hope.

Guard. It's your only chance.

L. Leslieson [*sitting down in despair on the box again*]. Oh, what a stupid people, what a barbarous country !

Andy [*in a rage now*]. A gay lot yous are yourselves, aren't yous ? Why th' hell didn't your great Foreign Office arrange to have a car waitin' at th' thrain to bring its High Official safe an' snug an' crowin' outa him to his great Prime Ministher ?

Guard. Yes, why didn't they ? Or send you down in a car straight to where you were goin' ?

Corny [*ejaculating*]. Hadn't th' wit !

Martha [*murmuringly from the window*]. Hadn't th' wit !

Sean [*to Lord Leslieson*]. Well, what are yeh goin' to do — chance th' creel-car or no ?

Corny [*quietly but significantly*]. I notice that you chaps haven't referred that question to me. It's one thing to want th' creel-car, another thing to get it.

Martha. Another thing to get it.

L. Leslieson [*suddenly jumping to his feet — with resolution*]. I'll chance it, I'll chance the donkey and the creel-car ! It will be a unique experience !

Sean [*with satisfaction*]. That settles it.

Guard. A happy endin'.

Corny. Yous are a bit quick, aren't yous ?   Settled, is it ?
Happy endin' no less, is it ?   Arranged right in front
of Cornelius Conroy's kisser without askin' him would
he or wouldn't he.

Martha. Would he or wouldn't he.

Sean. Be your silence, Corny, we thought you was
agreein' with us.

Guard. We did that.

Andy. It was natural.

Corny [*ominously*]. Yous did, did yous ?   Natural, was
it ?   [*Explosively*] Well, if your laddo wants to get
where he's goin' he'll damn well have to walk !

Martha. Have to walk.

Corny [*determinedly*]. I'm not goin' to harass little Jinnie
out of her well-earned sleep for that boyo, or for any
other laddo.   Jinnie isn't goin' to prowl about this
time o' th' night for anyone.

Guard [*testily*]. All right, all right !

Corny [*ignoring the interruption*]. I'm not goin' to rouse
little Jinnie out of her donkey-dhreams, no, not for
any England's great Prime Ministhers, or for any
sthruttin' High Official of England's Foreign Office !
[*More vehemently*] I'm tellin' yous I wouldn't molest
little Jinnie out of her present repose if it was th'
Parish Priest of Kylenamoe aself that was askin' me
to do it !

Andy. You can't expect th' poor man to walk there —
how could he know th' way ?

Corny. There's nothin' to prevent th' lot of yous, some in front, the others behind, goin' with him to bring him safely there.

Andy [*aghast*]. An' leave th' thrain standin' where she is?

Corny [*sarcastically*]. She must be gettin' used to it be now. [*As he ends, a little crowd of passengers, headed by a young woman, appear at the corner of Corny's hut. They stand there, all looking a little anxious and bewildered.*]

Woman Passenger [*in front of group*]. Th' passengers have asked me to inquire into th' motionless condition of th' thrain for near a half hour o' time? Th' poor passengers is furious! So yous had better pop back to your thrain at once without measurin' out any more of your parleyvoo.

Sean. Parleyvoo indeed! We're not doin' any parley-vooin', I'd have th' passengers know.

Guard [*indignantly*]. Pop back! Passengers' place is in th' thrain, an' as yous are undher my charge while yous are there, yous yourselves had betther pop back, for yous have no right to come infilthratin' here intherferin' with the duty of an Official gettin' a quantity of goods into safe supervision.

Sean [*taking the Guard up*]. To be despatched first thing in th' mornin' to th' consignees of th' town of Kylenamoe.

L. Leslieson [*suddenly jumping up — excitedly*]. There you are! You are concealing things from me! Off his guard, he blurted it out for all to hear!

Sean [*startled and puzzled*]. Blurted out what, man?

L. Leslieson [excitedly]. The town ! You said the town of
Kylenamoe ! I heard you ; we all heard you ! I must
get to it ! Do you hear ? — I must be directed to the
town !

Andy. Aw, sit down an' close your bake — we've another
question before us now !

Sean [to Lord Leslieson]. It's only a way o' talkin', man.
If you read the district journal tomorrow you'll see an
item sayin' that Yestherday, an important and heavy
consignment of goods reached th' town of Kylenamoe
from Dublin, and the Guard of the thrain and the
railway porthers were busy half th' night storin' them
to wait for delivery or collection, first thing in th'
mornin'.

L. Leslieson [sinking down on to the box again]. Oh my God !
Deceit and lies !

Woman Passenger [indignantly, almost passionately]. So this is
th' way yous waste our public money ! We'll soon lay
this kinda conduct low ! Th' one first-class passenger
left in th' thrain's busy at a Report of this terrible wait
in th' threat in the core of th' dead an' silent night.

Corny [soothingly]. Aysey, aysey ; subside, subside !

Martha [just as soothingly]. Subside !

*Woman Passenger [half up to Martha in the window and half
down to Corny at the door].* Subside yourselves ! Maybe
yous don't know that I have to get out at Kylenatoraf,
an', maybe, th' conveyance sent to bring me home'll
have got tired waitin', an' gone, so that I'll have to
trudge timid for eight miles through a dark an'
lonesome land !

L. Leslieson [*with resentful dismay*]. My God, it's all a dark and a lonesome land ! [*With sudden thought.*] I must see the Head Porter !

Woman Passenger [*venomously*]. Yous'll soon get what's comin' to yous, for our only first-class passenger's busy inditin' a Report of this petrifyin' delay at Kylenamoe to send to the Railway Authorities ; so yous'll soon be on th' carpet — th' lot of yous !

L. Leslieson [*slapping Sean on the shoulder*]. I must see the Head Porter !

Sean [*testily*]. Oh, quiet, man, quiet !

L. Leslieson [*emphatically*]. I demand to see the Head Porter !

Sean [*shouting angrily*]. You are seein' him : I'm th' Head Porter !

L. Leslieson [*as loudly as Sean*]. The Stationmaster, then ; I must see the Stationmaster !

Sean [*more loudly still*]. He's away — I'm th' Pro-Tem Stationmaster !

Woman Passenger. When're we goin' to start ? Th' man left on th' engine says th' whole thrain's swollen with anxiety to get goin' !

Sean [*suddenly aware of the train's delay*]. We're startin' now ! [*He darts into the hut and darts back, this time wearing a peak-cap with a faded gold band round it instead of the red-banded one he had worn before. To Andy O'Hurrie — with a hand-gesture towards where the train is*] What are you doin' here ? You've no right to leave your engine, Andy O'Hurrie !

Andy [*indignantly*]. You big mouth, you hurry-scurried me into delayin' !

Sean [*all business — to the passengers*]. Go on, yous, get back to your carriages ! At once ; go on ! [*The passengers hurry off. To the Guard*] You, too — What are yeh lingerin' here for ? Why aren't yeh on your way to Kylenatoraf ; on your way to Kylenatoraf ? What's that poor lady to do if th' conveyance doesn't wait for her, an' she has to toil eight miles through a dark an' lonesome land ? You're already half an hour late in your skedule !

Guard [*in full-blown anger*]. Yeh bog-born ignoramus, who're yeh talkin' to ! Imagine it, like o' you ordherin' one a Guard commandin' a main-line thrain, transposin' livin' souls from where they are to where they want to go, without a rib o' hair on one of them gettin' ruffled——

Sean [*interrupting*]. Well, betther start doin' it again !

Guard [*ignoring interruption*]. Stoppin' at Killcolm, Bally-funbarr, Kylenamoe, Kylenatoraf, Killcormac, an' all th' rest o' them, depositin' eager passengers without harm or threpidation !

L. Leslieson [*piteously*]. Well, why not deposit me without trepidation at Killnalayna House ?

Guard [*swiftly and irritably*]. Thrain doesn't go there, man !

Sean [*emphatically*]. There'll be a row about all this, an' yous can't say I didn't warn yous against gossipin', gossipin' here when yous should ha' been chee choo chee chooin' through th' rare or rough recesses of th' counthry !

Guard [*catching Andy by a sleeve — hurriedly*]. Hurry an' come on, Andy, an' leave this venomous talkative toad to croak in his own miry desolation !

Andy [*coolly*]. Stay put, Mick. We're all right. We'll settle this threatenin' jaytalker.

Sean [*imperatively*]. Go on, th' pair of yous, now, an' give your thrain a chance of arrivin' where it's supposed to go, before th' poor passengers dhribble away into old age !

Andy [*quietly*]. We can't go ; we daren't move.

Sean [*taken a little aback*]. Why th' hell can't yous ?

Andy. Because of the deliberate an' atrocious negligence of th' fella that's talkin' !

Sean [*taken aback more — suspicious*]. Me ?

Andy. Cornelius Conroy there sees it, Mrs. Martha Conroy sees it.

Corny [*shocked and resentful — not sure of what's coming*]. Me ? Eh, you're not goin' to dislocate me in th' tangle of your disputes. No, sir. I seen nothin' nor I heard nothin' either !
   [*He swiftly moves within, banging the door shut after him.*

Martha [*from the window*]. I seen nothin', heard nothin' either !
   [*She retires from the window, pulling it down with something of a bang, too.*

Sean [*jubilant*]. Aha, yous seen it, but Corny didn't, Martha didn't !

Andy [*disappointed but confident*]. You can see it yourself.

Sean. Your buttie, Michael Mulehawn's lookin' a bit puzzled. Tell us what it is, or are yeh outa your mind ?

Andy [*going closer to Sean — triumphantly*]. It's what prevented us from movin' all th' time, an' prevents us now, fool ! No engine-driver can go by it ; no ; he daren't pass a danger signal : th' Red Light stops him !

Sean [*swiftly glancing up at the signal, sees the Red Light — panic-stricken*]. Jasus !
  [*He dashes up the steps of the hut, and, after some moments, the clank of a lever is heard, and the Red Light turns to Green.*

Guard [*watching the signal*]. Ah, th' Green Light shows at last !

Andy. I had him there, th' turn-about, run-about bastard !

Guard [*briskly*]. Let's go — we're half an hour behind time.

Andy [*with assurance as they hurry out*]. Here goes to get to Kylenatoraf in good time, or end in Hell !
  [*Sean comes hurrying down the steps from the upper storey of the hut as the shrill whistle of the Guard is heard outside to the right, followed by the louder blast from the engine's siren. Then the cheh choo cheh choo of the train is heard as she pulls out, and the sound of her going fades away into the distance. Sean comes over to Lord Leslieson who is sitting dejectedly on the box, his head in his hands. Sean goes to hut slowly, and changes the light from green to red, lilting softly as he goes up and comes down :*
    Th' heart bow'd down be weight o' woe
    To weakest hopes will cling,

> To thought an' impulse while they flow
> That can no comfort bring.

Sean [*standing and looking towards where the train is travelling*]. Left me alone with you. Thinkin' of no one but themselves. Concenthrated may fane men ! [*He bends over Lord Leslieson.*] D'ye hear ? They've left us alone.

L. Leslieson [*looking up wanly at Sean*]. Thank God for that !

Sean [*lilting chorus as he goes over to Leslieson*].
> That can no comfort, no comfort bring.

[*Bending down closer to him.*] Eh, sir, you seen no Red Light, did yeh now ? [*Before Lord Leslieson can answer.*] No, of course not. Th' Green Light was goin' all th' time, wasn't it ; all th' time ?

L. Leslieson. It's here still.

Sean. What is ?

L. Leslieson. The Red Light — it shines over all this country !

Sean [*realising there's no help there*]. Well, what are you goin' to do ? I have to put th' box inta store.

L. Leslieson [*rising*]. Oh.
[*He goes back and squats on ground, leaning against the hut while Sean puts the goods into the little store-house.*]

Sean [*worried*]. You can't stay there all night, man. My place has only two rooms ; I'm but a lodger ; th' woman o' th' house spends herself mindin' a husband dyin' o' cancer.

L. Leslieson [*agonizedly*]. A country of desolation, of aimless chatter, dirt, and disease !

Sean [*persuasively — after a pause*]. Why not give a knock at the Conroys' opposite ? She keeps th' place shinin' and warm and dhry.

L. Leslieson. No, no, thank you`; I prefer the bare night.

Sean. If I was you, I would.

L. Leslieson [*tersely*]. You're not Me !

Sean. All right ; have it your own way. [*He moves off lilting*] :
>   The mind will in its worst despair
>   Still ponder o'er the past.
[*He comes back towards Leslieson. Anxious.*] I don't like leavin' you. [*A pause.*] I'll leave th' lanthern anyway ; it'll warm your fingers anyhow. [*He leaves the lantern a little way from Lord Leslieson.*] It'll keep yeh company anyhow. [*A pause.*] Well, good night. You've the moon with you, anyway, thank God. [*He pauses again, but as Lord Leslieson is silent, he goes slowly out. Lilting as he goes*] :
>   That can no comfort bring,
>   That can no comfort, no comfort bring.
[*After a few moments, the Conroys' window opens and Martha looks out at the figure huddled beside the hut. Then the door opens, and Corny stands there, looking, too, at the figure huddled in the corner. He goes over to it, and taps Lord Leslieson on the shoulder gently.*]

Corny [*gently but embarrassed, and getting it over quick, for he is shy at giving a favour*]. Yeh can't stay here all night. A fine moon in th' sky, God bless it ; yis. Th' missus's laid down a matthress before th' fire, an' I've piled it with sods so's it'll last th' night. Ay, indeed, a grand moon. Come on.

B.G.C.—L

L. Leslieson [*touched*]. That is kind of you, but I couldn't
——

Corny [*irritably*]. Yeh'll have to ! I can't have th' missus
pokin' me out every ten minutes to see if you're all
right — out an' in o' bed every five minutes ! A
breakfast of fresh eggs, home-made bread, an' lashin's
o' tea'll make a new man o' you.

L. Leslieson [*getting to his feet stiffly*]. Well, that's extremely
kind of you both. Thanks. I'll pay well for it.

Corny [*with dignity*]. You'll pay nothin' for it ! A friend
or enemy in disthress is welcome to share whatever we
have. Payment would put a black spot on God's
blessin'.

L. Leslieson [*surprised but a little awed*]. Yes, yes, I see.
I'm very grateful.

Corny. While you're gettin' breakfast down yeh, I'll
have th' creel-car an' Jinnie ship-shape for yeh, and
yeh can arrive where you're goin' gay an' gorgeous like
a King o' Burren.

L. Leslieson [*enthusiastic*]. I can ! Jinnie and the creel-car !
Real Irish !

Corny [*business-like suddenly*]. Betther know what you're
lettin' yourself in for.

L. Leslieson [*suspicious at once*]. Oh ! Yes ?

Corny [*firmly*]. I charge for th' hire o' th' car an' Jinnie ;
market price — five shillin's up to five miles, seven 'n'
sixpence up to seven, ten shillings up to ten ; so as
your place is only an inch or two from nine miles,
you'll have to fork out ten shillin's.

L. Leslieson [*highly relieved*]. Oh, of course, but too cheap
— say a pound.

Corny [*tersely*]. Ten shillin's th' market price.   We do
business here as th' market rules‚ without fear or favour
for party or person — see ?

L. Leslieson [*half-stunned*]. Quite.   Yes, of course.   Market
price.   Yes, yes.
   [*Mrs. Conroy has appeared at the door, and stands a
   matronly figure in the centre of the warm, golden glow
   flooding from the cosy, sheltering home.*

Martha [*stretching out her two hands in welcome*]. Come on in,
sir.   You're welcome, an' God save you kindly.

L. Leslieson [*very much moved*]. Thank you, thank you, an'
God save you and your good man kindly, too.
   [*They go in.   The door shuts slowly.   The forgotten
   lantern stands where it had been left, burning brightly.
   Away in the distance the faint sound of the engine's siren
   is heard, and*

THE PLAY ENDS

ACKNOWLEDGEMENT

' Love's old sweet song ' : music by J. L. Molloy ; words by E. Clifton Bingham. Copyright 1884 by Boosey & Company Limited. Reproduced by permission of the publishers, Boosey & Hawkes Limited, 295 Regent Street, London, W.1. All rights reserved.

MUSIC FOR THE INCIDENTAL
SONGS

BEHIND THE GREEN CURTAINS
I saw from the beach

1. I saw from the beach when the morning was shining A

bark o'er the wa - ters move glo - rious-ly on; I

came when the sun o'er that beach was de - clin - ing, The

bark was still there but the wa - ters were gone! I

came when the sun o'er that beach was de - clin - ing, The

bark was still there but the wa - ters were gone!

2. Ne'er tell me of glo-ries se-rene-ly a-dorning The
3. Oh who would not welcome that mo-ment's re-turning, When

close of our day, the calm eve of our night; Give me
pas-sion first wak'd a new life thro' his frame, And his

back, give me back the wild fresh-ness of Morn-ing, Her
soul, like the wood that grows prec-ious in burn-ing, Gave

clouds and her tears are worth Ev-'ning's best light, Give me
out all its sweets to love's ex - qui - site flame! And his

back, give me back the wild fresh-ness of Morn-ing, Her
soul, like the wood that grows prec-ious in burn-ing, Gave

clouds and her tears are worth Ev-'ning's best light.
out all its sweets to love's ex - qui - site flame!

FIGURO IN THE NIGHT
Oh, dear, what can the matter be

The hou-ses are emp-ty the night it is fall-ing, The

hou-ses are emp-ty the night it is fall-ing, There

is - n't a sin-gle bird ev - en left call-ing, Since

all have gone off to the fair.____

CHORUS

Oh dear, what can the mat-ter be, Dear, dear,

what can the mat - ter be, Oh dear,

what can the mat-ter be John-nie's so long at the

fair.____ My John - nie he wan - ted to

stay here and mind me But in what state of dress would me

ma 'n da find me, They'd hus - tle me in - to my

room and then bind me When they both hur - ried home from the

fair.____ I've prom - ised me heart a

time of good kiss - ing, I've prom - ised me heart a

time of good kiss - ing, With noth - ing that's live - ly and

love - ly left miss - ing When John - nie comes back from the

fair.____ Sweet A - lice, I've brought you the

bon - nie blue rib - bons For long in our coun - try so

rare.____ So op - en the door__ and

then you can dare me To tie up your bon - nie brown hair.__

Love's old sweet song

1. Once in the dear dead days be - yond re - call,
2. Ev - en to - day we hear Love's song of yore,

When on the world the mists be - gan to fall,
Deep in our hearts it dwells for ev - er - more

Out of the dreams that rose in hap - py throng
Foot - steps may fal - ter wea - ry grow the way

Low to our hearts Love sang an old sweet song;
Still we can hear it at the close of day,

And in the dusk where fell the fire - light gleam,
So till the end, when life's dim sha - dows fall,

Soft - ly it wove it - self in - to our dream.
Love will be found the sweet - est song of all.

Just a song at twi - light, when the lights are

low, And the flick - 'ring sha - dows soft - ly come and

go, Tho' the heart be wea - ry sad the day and

long, Still to us at twi - light comes Love's old

song, comes Love's old sweet song.

THE MOON SHINES ON KYLENAMOE
I dreamt I dwelt in marble halls

I dreamt I dwelt in mar-ble halls, With ves-sels an' serfs be me side____ An' of all who as--sem-bled with-in__ those walls, That I was the hope and pride____ I had rich-es too great to count, could boast Of a high an-ces-tral name____ I had rich-es too great to count, could boast Of a high an--ces-tral name.____

The heart bow'd down

1. The heart bow'd down by weight of woe To weak-est hopes____ will cling, To thought and im-pulse while they flow, That can no com - fort bring that can no__ com-fort, no com - fort bring. With these ex-cit-ing scenes will blend, O'er

plea - sures   path -   way thrown   But_____

mem-'ry is the   on - ly friend That grief can call__ its

own,   That grief can call its own,__   That_____

grief can call its own.   2. The mind will in its

worst de-spair Still pon-der o'er_____ the past.   On

mo - ments   of   de -   light that were   Too

beau - ti - ful_____   to last, that were too__

beau - ti - ful, too beau-ti - ful to last.   To

long de - part-ed years ex-tend No vis-ions with__ them

flown, For_____ mem-'ry is the   on - ly friend That

grief can call__ its own, That grief can call its

own,__   That_____ grief can call its   own!